I0213758

The Land My Childhood Knew

An autobiography

Mary June Flaiz Wilkinson

Coffee Table Books
an imprint of
GreenWine Family Books

The Land My Childhood Knew

Library of Congress Control Number: 2011928794
Wilkinson, Mary June Flaiz 1922 -
The Land My Childhood Knew
ISBN 978-1-935434-44-3

Subject Codes and Description:
1. BIO511000 Biography & Autobiography: Childhood Memoir 2. TRV003040 Travel: Asia-India 3. NAT001000 Nature: Animals - General

Cover Design by Shannon Payne

Published by
GreenWine Famiy Books
a division of
GlobalEdAdvance Press
www.gea-books.com

To the memory of my dearest friend
and the love of my life

Stan

Acknowledgement

Jim, our youngest boy and his family, lives on a hilltop right beside me. One day his middle boy, Andrew, asked me to do something interesting,

“Grandma, tell me a story—a story about when you were a little girl.”

Hearing the request, Jim added, “Yes! A story! Better than that - how great would it be if you’d write a book? With sixteen grandkids—you could just hand them one—and that would be it.”

“But, I’m so busy just now making picture albums for all of you kids.”

“You can do that – *after* you write the book.”

And so it was that Jim and Andrew inspired me to start writing. It has been a fun experience—filled with treasured memories.

Jim and Jen have been such sweethearts helping and encouraging me every step of the way. Jim as the overall director and Jennie have helped in many ways, mostly keeping me and my old computer going.

And, of course, there’s Randy–our second boy–and his daughter, Shannon. What a joy they have been. Randy by contacting the people who put it all together and Shannon designing and putting together the beautiful cover spread

—making it not just “out there” or too mystical—but rather just a good blend.

All of the other children have been great –each helping in their own way. I find it hard to thank them sufficiently for their participation.

Adding to this are our many family and friends who have kindly answered questions, brought up memories and contributed to the content of the book. I wish to thank you all for your time, thoughts, and prayers. It has been so greatly appreciated.

Introduction

Mary June Flaiz Wilkinson was born and spent her early years in British East India, living there while the Rajahs, wild animals, and the British still ruled the land.

In those days, only the Rajahs were allowed to own guns. So, from time to time, tigers and leopards would invade the villagers' livestock. And, on occasion, would even kill an innocent villager. It was during such experiences that Mary June's father, Ted Flaiz, the founder of a local school and hospital, would be called upon to save a village from these big cats. Reluctantly, (for he loved the wild life of India), he would kill these beautiful animals. But then, he would do whatever was necessary to protect his neighbors, his young family, and the success of his heavenly mission.

Throughout the following pages Mary June chronicles these days, when the love of family, the laughter of friends, and the lessons of life all wove together into a tapestry of memories, which began in the place she fondly calls, *' The Land My Childhood Knew.'*

~ one ~

Good-bye to My India

"I'll never forget India.
She will always be mine."

The deep-throated blast of the ship's horn told us that it was "Anchor's Away." Hanging onto the ship's railing, Ted and I peered below, scanning the crowd for two familiar faces. "Where were our friends, the Cooper boys?" Before mastering the gangplank we had assured them we would wave good-bye from the very top deck.

Feeling a tap on my shoulder, I turned to see a gentleman holding a tray of rolled up paper ribbons—all different colors. He smiled and held out the tray.

"What color of ribbon do you want, Missy? They're free."

Seeing my puzzled expression, he explained, "This is a game that everyone likes to play. You just take a hold of this end of the roll," he demonstrated with an exaggerated flair. "Then throw the other end to your friend below. When the ship pulls out, the ribbon unwinds. You must hang on as long as you can, for the last two people holding an unbroken ribbon wins the game. It's fun! You better try it."

Leaning over the tray, I searched for just the right color. Passing over the blues, browns, and tans I spotted a beautiful bright purple.

Realizing that Ted had missed out on the conversation I asked the man if he could have one, too. "Of course," he said and held out the tray for my older brother's inspection. A pretty green was his choice. We thanked the man and turned our eyes back to the dock.

"There they are!" Ted pointed below. "Just there...Doug and Danny!"

Following his finger, I picked them out of the crowd, along with their mom and dad standing behind them, all waving. But then everyone was. It was a sea of bobbing heads and outstretched arms, all playfully reaching for the sudden colorful rain of descending ribbons.

It was a happy good-bye party.

"Hurry up, Kids. Take good aim and toss 'em," Dad called out, standing just behind us with Mom.

Ted lined up the distance and threw as hard as his twelve-year-old arm could muster. In a slow motion blur, the roll unraveled as it sailed out and down toward the crowd on the dock. Holding his end tightly, he waited impatiently to see who would catch his offering. Although Doug was too far away to catch the other end, a boy of about 14 snagged the almost unraveled roll and waved it in triumph.

Stepping up to the railing I likewise launched my purple streamer. After playing on the breeze a moment, it too fell towards the dock. A tall man strained to catch it, but he fumbled the grab and the ball rolled, without fanfare into the sea.

"It's not fair," I pouted to Dad. "I wanted Danny to catch it! We didn't even have a chance."

In that moment of disappointment, my ears turned my attention to the parting messages being shouted from ship to shore and back again.

"Good-bye... God bless!"

"We'll see you next year..."

One or two even called, "See you in heaven!"

The fun part of the trip was beginning to take on a heavy tone—a touch of sadness. As I listened, an older lady standing next to me tried to out shout the crowd. I looked carefully to see who was holding her streamer. And there below, connected by a strand of twisted color, was a young woman with a man beside her. Together they were holding a big sign. But what did the sign say?

"It's too far away," I complained. "I can't read it."

Dad took the binoculars from around his neck and handed them to me. And aiming for the couple below, the blurred letters slowly came into focus:

Mom, We'll Love You Forever

Just then a gust of wind blew the sign from their hands. They scrambled for it, but it lifted over their heads and landed face down in the sea. Instinctively I looked up at the face of the mother. Was she feeling the pain of separation, too? The answer was flowing freely down her cheeks. And with a helpless little wave of her hand she bid good-bye to her kids, buried her face in a handkerchief, and turned from the railing.

Another blast from atop the ship signaled the huge engines were engaged. Instantly the sea around the ship came to life, bubbling, and churning furiously. The deck below our feet shuddered. And then, ever so slowly, the vessel christened *THE EMPRESS OF RUSSIA* began to drift away from land.

The space between the dock and the ship gradually grew wider. It all seemed exciting and fun... but now, I could see – my country was leaving me. *MY INDIA!*

For some time Ted's ribbon danced in the wind. But now, like the rest of the streamers, all of the strands were becoming thinner, tighter, as if they didn't want to let go of the shore. Soon they began to break and fall into the sea. One by one the colorful connections snapped. Ted leaned farther and farther over the railing. He was a competitive boy and was hoping desperately to keep his ribbon in the game.

"Take care, Buddy. Don't lean out any farther," Dad cautioned. "It's not worth the chance of a swim in the ocean."

Studying the situation carefully, he saw that his sliver of green was almost to the breaking point. That's when the notion hit him.

Sprinting off towards the stern of the ship, he hugged the railing, dodging a few surprised pedestrians along the way. The move bought him some time.

I counted one... two... only three streamers were left. Now all eyes were riveted on the match. Who was going to win?

On the dock below, I saw the boy - Ted's connection. He was fighting his way to the dock's end. That, too, would add a few more seconds.

Then, out of the corner of my eye, I saw a bright orange ribbon snap and dive to its death in the churning waters below. Now we were down to two.

"Hey, you with the green streamer," a voice in the crowd yelled, "you're doin' great!"

I stole a glance at Ted. He was enjoying all of the attention.

"Keep it up! Keep it up!" called another.

There was suddenly a swell of hand claps and whistles.

"Don't let go. Don't let it break."

It seemed that all of the cheering was focused on Ted.

The only other ribbon up now was being held by a man dressed in a strange costume—a bright flowered shirt atop a bright colored skirt. Maybe he was a South Pacific native. I looked down to see who was holding the other end. Following the streamer down, I spotted a pretty young lady dressed in the very same colorful, happy outfit. But she was holding a handkerchief to her nose and wiping her eyes.

At that moment the green streamer broke!

A loud collective sigh came from the crowd. "Oh nooooooooo. Poor boy." The ribbon had broken up at Ted's end of the roll. For a moment it fluttered above the churning water. Then, despite all of Ted's efforts, the streamer spiraled into the depths, below the ship's wide wake.

Now only one streamer remained, dancing on the wind.

I hesitantly ventured a look at my brother's face, for I knew its countenance would spell disappointment. He had lost by one ribbon. Just one!

Quite far away now, the boy who had held the other end waved to Ted. He waved back... but not as energetically.

As my eyes veered off, I noticed another boy. It was Doug! His hands were cupped around his mouth. Was he trying to tell us something?

"Look Ted! It's Doug," I pointed below. "He's trying to say something!"

Above the din and distance of the occasion we strained to listen. Ted cupped his hand over his ear.

"Pretty good, Ted. You almost won." He was shouting at the top of his lungs, "Salaam. Salaam."

"Salaam, Doug!" Ted yelled, waving with all his might. "See you in America."

And with the snap of a ribbon and a final wave, our last connection with the land my childhood knew was severed.

* * *

In silence our family stood at the railing—each deep into his or her own thoughts. Why was I so sad?

Turning around I looked for Mom.

Whenever I was struggling with what I thought was a heavy burden of some kind, my mom always had a way of lessening the load; she had a knack for tossing away the unnecessary. She didn't just instinctively push them out of the way, but rather with logic and understanding she would reason through each problem. And before I knew it, my heart was happy and light again.

Now, seeing my tear stained face, Mom reached down and squeezed my hand. "We'll be back in a minute."

Sending Dad a knowing glance, she led me to a nearby bench, and we sat down. Looking up at Mom, I was surprised to see that her eyes were likewise brimming with tears.

Somehow the moment seemed too special—too holy to interrupt with common talk. So we sat for a few moments in silence—maybe five minutes. Then, breaking the stillness, she offered, "Honey, I know exactly how you feel."

"You do?"

"Leaving India, for you, is like saying good-bye to one of your dearest friends. Now everything that you do, see, or experience will be judged by your love and understanding of India."

A light breeze swept across the deck, brushing a lock of Mom's hair onto her face. She pushed it back and continued, "It was fourteen years ago—a foggy day in December that Dad and I sailed out of the Seattle harbor for India."

"How old were you?" I asked.

"Nineteen...Dad, twenty-two. So you can see, Honey, we went through the same feelings of separation then that you are going through now. And we had to say good-bye to both dads and moms, brothers and sisters, too."

"Everything seems so sad," I sniffled. "Did it take very long to get happy again?"

"I will have to say that it did take quite awhile. But you know what?" With a glint in her eye, she forced a smile. "I have a secret – a little hint that I have found very helpful. Want me to share it?"

"Oh, please do."

Mom readjusted her position on the bench and stared ahead. With a far away and long ago look in her eyes she began.

"Always keep in your heart a little spot reserved just for your childhood memories of India," she confided. "Keep them protected, well hidden so that when you get lonesome for those happy days of long ago you can right away remember, and be happy again." And with that she leaned over and gave me a hug. Then we sat for awhile in silence, watching the long wake of the ship push us ever further from the shore. Then... "Mom, if someone asks me 'What is your country?' I can just say 'India' and that would be right, wouldn't it?"

Ted, June, Punkie, Freddie

"Of course, Honey. India will always be yours. But you need to remember that we are on our way to a new country now. And someday you may find that you have pretty much forgotten about India. Then it will be America. America."

"No, Mom. I'll never forget India. She will always be mine."

* * *

We sat for some time watching the sea gulls gliding above the deck–dipping and soaring. The decibel level was mighty high as they scrapped and fought over the little tidbits being thrown to them. Dad had told us that the gulls would be keeping us company until we got far out to sea. I was glad to hear that. I liked them. They were fun to watch.

"Missy, can I interest you in some lemonade?"

Turning around I recognized Aziz, the ribbon man. But this time he was holding another tray – full of ice cold drinks.

"Would Missy's mother care for a drink, too?" Aziz smiled at Mom.

"Oh yes, of course," Mom nodded.

As he and his tray walked away, I watched him go.

"What a nice man," I mused. "Most grown up big men don't bother to talk to kids like me."

After a while Mom decided that it was time to go below. We would be on board for some time and she was anxious to get things in order.

"Think I'll go below. Get the place settled," Mom hinted. "Got any takers?"

"You got me," Dad chimed in.

"Not me," answered Ted, still gazing over the railing. "I want to stay here just as long as I can see India."

"Me, too," I smiled up at Mom. She understood.

As our parents disappeared behind the big swinging doors, Ted and I stared back at the shore.

"Sorry you lost the ribbon game," I offered. "It was soooo close."

"Yeah," my brother's shoulder dropped.

For a long time, we stood and watched the slip of land get smaller and dimmer.

"Hey, Sis, do you remember what Dad told us about our topis?" he gestured to the round, box-like hats atop our heads. "We won't be using them much longer. They don't wear them in America...What do you say we donate them to India? It seems like we should honor India by giving it something that really meant something to us. I can't think of anything else to give."

With that, we both took off our topis, examining them from every angle. What memories they brought back!

Most of our childhood Ted and I had scampered about barefooted –shoes were just too much of a bother. Focusing my attention on the special pins stuck into the front rim of my topi, I remembered how we had "borrowed" them from Mom's sewing basket. The long slivers had been our clever solution to extend our outdoor time: When faced with a splinter in our feet, it was much easier to sit down right there with mom's pin and dig it out. Going all the way back to the house for the "surgery" lost us too much play time.

"So, how do we "donate" them–just sling them over the railing?"

"No," he shook his head. "Not enough *tamasha."* (Telegue for excitement). See all this khaki ribbon wrapped around the base? Let's just take hold of the end of the ribbon and then throw it over. Watch it unwind."

Pulling out his pocket knife from his pocket, he flipped it open and used its sharp wedge to locate the ribbon's beginning.

"Hey," I realized, "it's kinda like the ribbon game!" Finding the ends of both ribbons, he handed me mine.

"Here, hold the end real tight and then throw the topi out just as far as you can."

Summoning all my strength, I threw my voice out over the ocean, "Here's to India!" I then launched my hat over the railing, into the sky.

"Good-bye, topi." I called after it. "Thanks for taking care of me for all that time."

The colorful box-like head dress bounced and dived in the wind all the while unwinding as it dropped. Down, down it went. Then, like a huge monster the churning water gobbled it up. I felt the ribbon in my hand go limp.

Ted's topi followed in the same pattern, though for quite some time we were able to see it bobbing up and down, in and out of the churning water below.

Like the small slip of land which we had so desperately been holding in our view, both our hats and our homeland disappeared into the mists of ocean foam and distance. We were finished. Our vigil was over. We had honored our India.

"Good bye, India," Ted called into the blowing wind. "We'll see you again.......some time........I hope."

Front row: Emma Hughes, Mom, Maude Coyne, Junie and Punkie
Back row: Mr. Roa, Dad, Ted, The Rajah, Dr. Coyne and Freddie

Wedding portrait of The Rajah's daughter, Butchi.
The groom's father was also a Rajah.

~ two ~

Out There… What is it?

Closer and closer we came,
taking turns with the field glasses.

I opened my eyes the next morning to a world drenched in sunshine. From my upper berth I looked out of the porthole window at a sea that stretched on forever, with not so much as a ripple to destroy its glass like reflection.

"Anyone want to join me in a hike?" It was Dad calling out, looking for recruits on another of his adventures. Mom decided to pass on this one. Another time she would go. "I'll give you a half hour to get ready."

Although it took us the normal amount of time to take our showers, brush our teeth, make our beds, and have morning worship, that half hour seemed to take forever – cause an adventure was waiting.

Finally, as we waved good-bye to Mom and started out the cabin door, we bumped into Aziz, the man with the ever-present trays. Tall, lean, with mocha- chocolate skin, he greeted us with a toothy grin of recognition and bowed.

"I will be your steward for this trip."

Then glancing down to Ted and me he added, "If you two would like to play games, all children will be playing "Gotcha" from 9 to 11 this morning out on deck one."

"Gotcha?" Ted repeated. "How is it played?"

"With a big straw-filled ball." He gestured with his hands. "But that's all I'm going to tell you," he smiled, "'cause it's so much fun to learn as you go - and it's a good way to make new friends."

At the moment my mind flashed, "...friends...oh no I forgot!" And with that I turned and dashed down the long hallway, leaving everyone in my wake with a look of bewilderment.

Returning to the group a few minutes later, huffing and puffing, I struggled to catch my breath and explain at the same time.

"K-k-ketchup," I gasped.

Their bewilderment slipped into confusion.

"I forgot to bring Ketchup," I held her up for all to see. Old and held together with threads, string, and pins, I stroked her blond locks and continued. "I promised her last night that she would go with me on any hikes I might take."

Ted rolled his eyes.

Despite my brother's amusement, I considered Ketchup my greatest joy, coming to me when I was but three years old, a gift from my uncle and aunt in America. She was a truly beautiful doll—long blond hair—lightly curled. Her eyes—sky blue—closed when lying down but slowly opened when picked up. She had been promised a face lift when we get to America, along with a general make over. To me she was a really true person. So now that our foursome was present and accounted for, we nodded to Aziz and started up the stairs to the main deck.

As we stepped out into the morning light, the salty ocean spray was refreshing. "To get our proper amount of exercise for the day, I suppose that we'll have to do a little repeat walking," Dad surmised, his eyes scanning our mid-ship location. "But I bet you we will be seeing a lot of interesting things on the way."

Giddy at the possibilities, Ted, Ketchup and I played 'follow the leader.' The first thing that caught our attention was the ship's lifeboats, attached to the deck and hanging from sturdy, individual wenches. In case of fire on board or worse, these life boats would be lowered into the sea. The passengers would then quickly scramble down rope ladders into them. Dad explained that all ships were required to have enough life boats to hold all the passengers on board.

"You'll get a chance to see just how it all works," Dad added. "Before we get to Marseilles, I'm sure we'll have a fire drill."

As Dad continued to explain the workings of the ship, I could see the adventure in Ted Junior's eyes. Behind his gaze, my brother was no doubt scampering up and down those rope ladders, fighting off pirates, as the hero-Captain of his own sea-fairing frigate.

It was early morning. Cleaning crews were out scrubbing the deck and swabbing the chairs. As I studied their diligence, I noticed that two sea gulls were watching as well, gliding on the wind just off the ship's railing. It appeared that, like the ship's crew, these Bombay twins were scanning the deck, looking for an opportunity to do some cleaning of their own.

It was amusing to watch them squabble over a discarded piece of cookie. And I found myself hoping they would follow us all the way to France.

"I am going to call them 'Spic' and 'Span,'" I announced, noting the identifying black spot on his – Spic's side.

"Hey! Look! Look!" Ted shouted, breaking my trance. "Flying fish!"

Leaving the sea gulls I ran to the railing. Sure enough– there were fish suspended in mid flight above the waves, like they were competing in a race. Then I heard Dad call to us from further up deck.

"You guys like to see this huge ship slicing through the water?" he teased, pointing toward the ship's bow. "It's quite a sight."

Taking the bait, Ted ran past Dad, to where the two sides of the vessel converged. Once there, the 12 year old leaned on the railing and peered over, way over. "Sis, c'mon! You gotta see this!"

Standing next to Ted, I held tight to the railing and peered over the side. The sight was both mesmerizing and frightening.

From my vantage point I could look straight down and actually see both sides of the ship as it sliced through endless tons of water.

Behind us Dad lifted his field glasses from around his neck and started searching the ocean for anything of interest. "The water today is very unusual. It is almost always on the move. White caps as far as the eye can see. But today it's like glass, as far as one can - - Hey, what's this?"

"What? What do you see?" Ted impatiently reached for the glasses.

After a tense moment Dad handed Ted the binoculars and pointed to a distant dot in the sea. "I see it! How far away do you think it is?"

Shading his squinting eyes, Dad estimated, "I'd say about five miles."

Next was my turn with the glasses. And refocusing the image, the dark bobbing mass appeared to be a big log.

"Wish that it was more in the line of travel. We'll miss it by quite a bit."

No sooner than Dad finished his sentence, we felt the huge vessel slowly turn to the left. Leaning over the side, he looked back at the ship's wake. It was curving. The churning bubbles of foam confirming that we were headed directly for the object. No doubt the Captain was curious, too.

What a position to be in: a front row seat to a great play. Excitement was running high. I was jumping up and down. Ted and I were hoping for a whale. "If it's a whale," Dad cautioned, "it's probably asleep."

Closer and closer we came, taking turns with the field glasses.

It wasn't a log. Not a whale. Whatever it was, the object was lying cross-wise to the ship's line of travel. And if he didn't move and move quickly, there would be a heavy price to pay. The moment was so intense that no one spoke. Nearer and nearer it came.

Finally, the impact! But there was barely a shudder. The ship's hatched-like bow sliced through the large fish, tossing half of its body to one side, and the other bloody half in the opposite direction.

The surrounding sea turned an odd shade of pink, then dissipated, as if nothing out of the ordinary had happened at all. Afterward, the massive ship slowly returned to its original course.

Later, Aziz told us that a ship's officer had explained to him that the victim had been a huge shark, probably a white shark. And no doubt a sick or wounded one.

It was as if the ship, like my twin gulls, was doing its part to clean up the scraps, making everything spic and span.

~ *three* ~

Party Time

"...you know a real Rajah!?"

At supper that evening one of the ship's officers made an announcement. "From now on the young people on board will be eating their evening meals ahead of their parents. All children will meet in the dining room for their supper, and all adults will have their evening meals at eight o'clock. That way all moms and dads can get their little ones to sleep on time, and they can then be free to enjoy the evening as they wish."

There was wide spread clapping of hands from the adults, followed by a low groan of *"Nooooo!"*" from the children.

The officer, who seemed in fine spirit, then added, "Now you children—I have some good news for you. Tomorrow night you will have a really fun party right here in this big dining room."

Now it was the children's turn to clap.

"We call it the Welcome Party—welcome to this big ship—the Empress of Russia," he smiled. "There will be an extra special supper with ice cream and cake! But we ask only one thing...Each of you is coming from such interesting countries. So, we want you to represent your country in what you wear to the party, the more colorful the better. And, if you can say a few words about your country, that would be really special.

"We will have five judges sitting up here on the stage. They will evaluate all of the presentations and choose the one that they think is best. The boy or girl that wins will be given a prize—one that will be well worth working for! So thank you—we'll see you then."

And with that he bowed and left the dining room.

"Mom! Mom!" I shook her arm. "Remember the outfits that the Rajah gave us just before we left Nuzvid? I hope! Oh, I do hope we have them with us. Did you send them on ahead?"

"Yes, they are with us, Honey, and I think that they would be great for you and Ted to wear to the party."

"Oh Mom, I'm so excited!"

"Settle down," Ted moaned. "You're embarrassing me." I gave him a withering look and continued tugging Mom's arm towards our cabin.

From under one of the berths Mother pulled out a suitcase, and sure enough there they were—the beautiful white and gold clothes that we had just been talking about. As I lifted them out of the suitcase I remembered back to the day at the Rajah's palace in Nuzvid when the Rajah's wife, The Rani, took Mom and me to their enormous storerooms of clothes. Cupboards and shelves, shelves and cupboards all full of the most beautiful saris, blouses, and shawls. Another room was nothing but slippers, regular and bejeweled. And in their jewel room was a special cupboard containing a huge emerald set in a necklace. The Rajah explained to Ted and me how a battle was fought over that one emerald, and how his side had won, thereby securing for his family that beautiful jewel.

Gesturing to the room, The Rani invited both Mom and me to help ourselves to any of the clothes that took our fancy.

Mom pulled me aside and whispered in my ear. "Hold it down to just one outfit, June. O.K.? No more!"

I found that difficult to do. And it took me a long time to make up my mind. There were just too many beautiful clothes, but finally I decided.

I chose a wispy silkish white sari with bright gold thread embroidered into a design framing the edge of the sari. To this I added a beautiful white silk blouse trimmed in gold embroidery and then white leather slippers with gold studs sprinkled lavishly on top.

"Some time you may want a belt over the sari, Junie. So pick yourself a pretty one." The Rani then opened up a closet full of beautiful belts, some encrusted with eye catching jewelry, but I chose a gold one to go with the gold trimmings of my new sari.

"I'll never win the contest, Mom, but at least the people will see how pretty Indian clothes really are."

The night dragged by. Thoughts of the coming party were nudging out those of sleep. Finally morning dawned, and I heard Mom telling me to go down the hall to the bathroom to take my morning bath. I grabbed my bathrobe and towel and headed out the door.

"Good morning, Missy." Aziz called out. "How are you today?"

"Just fine, thank you," I answered, continuing on down the hall.

"Just a minute, Missy, I need to ask you a question." I slowed down and backed up a few paces.

"I was just wondering if you are a big enough girl to keep a secret - a really special secret." Aziz put his fingers to his smile and pretended to lock his lips.

"Never, never tell?" he whispered.

"Never. Never."

"All right, I'll trust you. But see that you never ever ever let me down. Promise?"

"Promise."

Motioning me down the hallway he pointed. "Do you see the little cubbyhole in the wall—there, on the right side?"

"Yeah."

"Every morning on your way to wash up, I want you to look in that little cupboard. In there you will find a present from me—something to enjoy while taking your bath. The fun secret starts this morning so be sure to look in the cubbyhole just now as you pass by."

"Well, thank you, Aziz. It's so nice of you."

With a playful grin Aziz watched as I approached the cubbyhole, put my hand in, and pulled out a nice big orange. Holding the gift up high, I waved it. Aziz acknowledged and waved back.

Munching on the orange—while sitting in the nice warm water—I pondered the question of Aziz and his secret. "Just to think that a big man like Aziz would take the time to have a secret with me. He's really a nice man! I can hardly wait to share the story with Mom. She will be so – Oh wait! I promised not to tell anyone. That means Mom, too, I guess."

The thought made me a little uneasy. I had always shared with Mom all that happened to me. "But a promise is a promise," I reasoned. That's what big people do—keep their word. They don't go blabbing everything they know. I want to show Aziz that I'm a big girl and can keep promises. And with that resolve, the question was settled.

At lunch, Mom suggested to Ted and I that we be at the cabin an hour before party time. "It may take awhile to get you both dressed and ready with some answers to questions they may ask you on stage."

"Say, Mom...I've decided I'm not going to do that dress-up thing tonight," Ted announced.

Mom looked disappointed. "You're not? Why, Honey? You've got such a great outfit."

"I know. But it's just too sissified. Too embarrassing."

"Are you sure? Remember that the winner gets a prize."

"Don't care. I just don't want to be called a sissy."

Knowing not to say any more, Mom quietly added some finishing touches to my costume, and then turned me around to face the family.

"Honey, you look like an absolute angel in all of that fluffy white silk and sparkling gold."

Growing up in India where women were always looked down upon had begun to rub off on me. She recognized this attitude, and so at every occasion where she could Mom tried to elevate my own vision of self worth.

* * *

From every direction came children dressed in elaborate costumes. The whole dining room was festooned with fairy like decorations. Banners were hanging from the walls–Burma, China, Malay, India, etc. By now Ted was rethinking his choice. Maybe it wouldn't have been so bad to dress up after all; the other boys dressed in costumes all looked to be having a great time.

"If all those children who plan to be a part of the competition tonight would please line up on this side of the stage we can get started on the program."

I looked up to see who was talking. It was the same ship's officer who the day before had announced the party. "Those of you who are not taking part please find your seats at the tables." The ship's band whipped up a lively tune, and the kids started tapping their toes to the beat of the music.

June and Ted

All of this *tamasha* was starting to get to me.

"Mom...I don't think I wanna do it now."

"Oh, Honey, of course you do. Just

keep your thoughts on the prize, and you'll come through fine."

I wasn't at all so sure but just then I found myself being swept along with the crowd–thirty to thirty five of them. I gave Mom a shy little good bye wave and headed for the stage. Suddenly I became aware that someone was reaching for my hand. I caught it and held fast. I recognized it to be Marilyn-the girl from Bangkok. She lived just down the hall and had spoken to me a few times since being on board. She looked and sounded as frightened as I was. But it was comforting now to know that I had a friend–someone who was going through the same scary situation.

The children were lined up. Then a man with paper and pencil went to each one asking two or three questions of each.

"What country do you represent? What can you tell us about this pretty outfit you have on?"

When it came my turn, I took a deep breath and began, "My country is India, a...n...d...," my voice started trailing off. Realizing my nervousness, the man kindly stepped in to help. "Did you buy your costume at a bazaar?"

"Oh no, " I answered. "Th....Th...The Rajah gave it to me. "

"The Rajah? You mean to tell me you know a real Rajah!?"

"He's my friend."

"Wow! That sounds like it would be an interesting story. Sometime you'll have to share it with me. Thank you, Junie." And with that he proceeded on down the row.

After a few nervous minutes, there was a sudden flourish of music by the band–then silence, as the Master of Ceremonies stepped to the microphone.

"Alice Butler, would you please come and join me."

A pretty girl walked slowly down and stepped onto the stage. Her long hair was lightly curled and powdered with a silver dust. Her "dress" was floor length and accented in silver trimming.

"Obviously you are representing a high class lady at a classy occasion, Alice. But don't tell me. Let me guess. I'll bet that you are here from...Let's see... Burma, right?"

"Right," answered Alice, and she stepped off the stage.

The children were all lined up according to alphabet, and I could see my turn coming soon. Horrors. I wasn't sure that I could survive the ordeal.

"Next, we have... Rosie. Rosie Dover."

All eyes were now fastened on the stage. "Where do you come from in this strange getup Rosie? I'll bet you didn't wear this fuzzy fur hat just to try and stay warm on the ship?"

"No," she answered with a friendly smile. "I was just trying to show everyone what we wear in Tibet. In the winter time that is, this hat and this coat, too.'"

"What a dreary place to live!" exclaimed the MC. "By the way, Rosie, what brought you to Tibet in the first place?"

"It was the Bible," she answered thoughtfully.

"How's that?"

"Well, somewhere in the Bible – don't know where just now – but it says that we need to tell everyone in the world about the gospel. And then Jesus will come. Dad and Mom read that verse and thought the people of Tibet should hear about it."

"Good for them," answered the MC. He then called up five more kids to interview.

I held my breath. Should I take this chance to run and disappear? That would end all the misery. But...too late. I heard my name echo over the dining hall speakers.

"Junie Flaiz." My heart beat wildly as I carefully climbed the stairs to the stage.

"Junie, could you please tell all these folks what country you are from and how you came across this pretty outfit." I tried hard to calm my fears and sound perfectly natural.

"I'm from India, down in south India. And this sari and blouse 'n other things were given to me by the Rajah of Teleprole."

"Am I right in calling him a friend of yours?"

"Yes. He is."

I answered many questions of interest to the MC. Then it was the next one's turn. I left the stage much relieved to be through with my part. Mom welcomed me to the table with a hug and a smile.

"What a great job, Honey. I'm proud of you."

The interviews were finished. All had been given the opportunity to represent their country. "And now comes the excitement—Who wins the prize?"

Through the entire program the five judges had been sitting at the back of the stage. Now one rose to the microphone.

"Anyone have a guess?" the judge asked playfully. "No? Well, let's see how the votes went. We have three prizes, and it looks like the number three prize goes to Charles from Korea. Number two –to Barbara from Cambodia... and the number one–first prize goes to....to......to.....to Junie from India!"

There was clapping and general "yahooing!" I could hardly believe what I had heard, and questioned Mom to see if it was really true.

The three winners were then called to the stage to collect their prizes. Charles was handed a beautiful gold box of Belgium chocolates–two pounds. Barbara was awarded three pounds of chocolates, and Junie–a beautiful five pound box of chocolates.

"It must have been that beautiful angel's outfit, Junie. Take good care of it and congratulations," the judge winked. I kindly thanked the MC and the judges. Then I hurried to my family to offer them a piece of my prize.

Following dinner Dad, Mom, Ted, and I headed for our cabin. It was a lovely evening, balmy and relaxed. There were the twins sitting on the railing–Spic and Span, my seagulls. They seemed happy, too. No grouching, just a little gentle nuzzling. All seemed well.

We all started down the stairs.

As we neared the front door, I noticed that someone was there–as though waiting for us to come. It was our smiling steward.

"How 'bout a piece of candy, Aziz?"

"Actual...real...candy?" With a genuine excitement he examined the box for the very best piece of chocolate.

"This is a big treat, Missy. We almost never get any candy here."

"Take another one, Aziz – Hope you'll like them."

~ four ~

Danger Onboard

"He needs to go to jail right now!
Do they have a jail on this boat?"

The early morning began with a bang. Worship (a time each morning and evening that we set apart to talk to God)...Our "repeat walk" around the deck... Breakfast... Then, a game of 'Gotcha!'

"How can I work all of these things into my program?" I wondered. But the morning slid by and before I knew it, the sun was high in the sky. It was Gotcha time.

Eric, the boy from Thailand, started the game. Stamping his feet, to get the blood flowing, he got into position and was ready to start.

"OK. Everybody. Let's go."

The straw-filled ball game continued for about an hour, when I became aware of someone standing on the sidelines. It was Aziz. Our steward was looking directly at me, and I reciprocated with a little wave of my hand.

Summoning me with a quirk of his finger, I came running. "What's up, Aziz?"

"It's so hot. I thought you might like some cold grape juice," he answered, motioning me to follow. "We can go down to the dining room and get some."

"That would be great," I sighed, wiping my brow. "Lead the way."

Aziz opened the big double doors, and we descended the stairway. Down. Down. I could barely see down here with the lights all turned off.

I noted that the chairs were all turned upside down on the tables and for direction I needed Aziz's hand. Leading me to the large sink cupboards, he put his hands under my arms and lifted me up onto the counter, then moved in the darkness to the sink to get the grape juice.

Swinging my dangling feet back and forth, without a care in the world, I was happy: happy that I was soon to be greeted by a cold drink–happy that I was on a short break from the upstairs game, just happy to be alive.

Then—suddenly—I felt this powerful force hit me from behind. It was like the bow of the ship slicing through the water - through that fish.

Somehow Aziz had managed to get himself behind me and on his knees had plunged his two fists down the front of my neck–inside of my dress!

Startled, I grabbed at my scattering, fleeing reason. But with no time to think it through I clutched at the solid flat surface below me, and pushed myself off of the counter. This left Aziz with nothing to hold on to. Sliding out of his control, I hit the carpet running - screaming at the top of my lungs, afraid with every stumbling step that a strong arm was about to grab me from behind. It was an uphill climb but reaching the top step, I pushed open the big swinging doors - and ran.

Dad and Mom looked up in time to see their frightened daughter burst through the cabin door and drop onto her bed.

"What!? What's wrong?" Mom's voice seemed far away. Seeing my disheveled look, she stood frozen momentarily stunned by the wild look in my eyes. Then coming to herself, Mom shook me.

"What is it? What's happened? Junie!?"

Reaching for Ketchup, I held her close, and slowly, ever so slowly the story spilled out. “Why would Aziz do that to me?” My eyes pleaded with Mom for an answer. “I thought that he was such a nice man.”

Pacing the floor, Dad started to piece the situation together. “Aziz would not have allowed her to go free. He would, no doubt, have taken Junie to his room, sedated her, and kept her hidden until dark, when he could have tossed her overboard. And no one would have been the wiser.”

“I won’t ever be able to look at that man, again. What was he planning on doing to my child anyway?” Mom’s face flushed. She was ready to throw Aziz overboard herself. “He needs to go to jail right now. Do they have a jail on this boat?”

“All I know is that it would be best if we didn’t do anything about it now. I’m sure that he won’t be working on our floor tomorrow. We can’t let Junie out of our sight from now on.”

Turning towards me and Ketchup, Dad added, “Either Mom or I will have to be with you whenever you leave this room. OK June? And when we get to Marseille I will report the incident to the authorities, and they can take care of the matter.”

It was decided that I would have to go to the adult meals and this arrangement would include Ted also.

The next morning when I headed to the bathroom, Mom was in tow and there was no Aziz decorating the hallway.

I looked in to the secret cubbyhole. Might there be just possibly a secret transfer from Aziz—a final good-bye? A final thank you? There was nothing but a confidence, an innocence...lost.

~ *five* ~

A Secret Message

"So what shall we say to Mr. Mussolini?"

The next day shone bright and clear. It had gone much like the previous ones. It was now afternoon and time for us to come in for a nap. We left the Gotcha game and got a good drink before settling down for a leisurely snooze.

"Hey, Hon. Wait a minute," Dad called to Mom from across the room. "Let me see that." I looked up to see what had intrigued Dad so, and saw a little tin jar in Mom's hand. She was just about to throw it out of the porthole window.

"What? This?" she questioned, tossing the jar to Dad.

"How 'bout you kids giving me a little help." The tone of adventure in my father's voice was unmistakable.

"Look out that window, Ted. What do you see...in the distance?"

"Well, I see some mountains, far away."

"That land is called Italy. It's being ruled over by a brute of a man named Mussolini. Let's write him a little note. Maybe it will get to him. Maybe it won't. Anyway, I think it would be kinda fun."

Gathering up a tablet and a pen, he added, "So, what shall we say to Mr. Mussolini? How about.... 'We think you're doing a terrible job of running Italy. Just look at the poor people who live in the slime of.....Noooooo.....can't write that! We can think of something better to say."

Sitting back in his chair Dad pondered the problem further. "Let's see... Maybe it would be better if we framed it this way: "Dear Mr. Mussolini, King George and I have been talking over the subject of buying Italy from you. If you think this a good idea, please write to Swini and go to Guini."

"Begs on throwing the can out of the window," I called out.

The note was stuffed into the tin can, and then closed tightly. Then, with all of my might I threw it out of the porthole and watched it bounce here and there on the sea.

"That will be the last time that we see you, Mr. Letter," Ted offered with a salute. Then turning to Dad he said, "How far away from land are we? Give me a guess."

Peering out the porthole to the distant purple mountains, he paused thoughtfully. "I'd guess we're about 20 miles from there."

Looking out of the small window I let my mind imagine all of the interesting things that the tin can would get to see, bouncing around out there in the ocean: Porpoises would give it a nudge wondering the little tin's purpose...Or maybe a flying fish would see its shiny allure and jump an extra wave to get a closer look. Whatever the little bottle's fate.... I hoped that one day it, too would find its way to shore, be discovered, treasured...and read.

The story carries on but first the message needs to share a little detour. 'Twas a year and a half later. We were living in Loma Linda, Calif. Dad and we kids were up at the library to pick up Mom from work when Dad gave out a laugh and said, "Well, what do we have here?" Ted and I came running. There on the front page of the daily Los Angeles newspaper was the startling headline: "Strange note washed up on southern shore of Italy." In pick-me-up language the writer tossed the words around having fun with his job. He told of a fisherman finding a can on the beach. In the can was a note. He realized that the verbage was all in English so he took it to the local magistrates who in turn sent it on to Rome. When it reached Mussolini, the short article declared, the president had a good laugh about the mysterious message that had washed up on his southern shore.

~ *six* ~

Strange Fire

People were pushing out of their doors,
and over each other,
all running for the top deck.

Our Gotcha game had been going strong for about two hours when we heard an odd shout from the other side of the deck.

"What's that?"

The game stopped, and everyone curiously ran to the north side of the ship. There, off in the distance, we could see why the lady clutching the railing had shouted. About five miles up ahead was a large mountain that looked to be on fire. Rivers of flame were rolling down its sides. And rising from it were dark billows of smoke, as if the mountain was an enormous chimney.

What a sight! It was almost dusk, and the subdued sky and dark water added to the overall effect. As the ship steamed nearer the site, the *hissing* sound of the lava hitting the ocean was unmistakable. It was as if we were sailing past the very gates of purgatory.

A ship's officer had grabbed a foghorn and said, "The mountain is called Stromboli." Ted was so taken by this sight that he chose to stay on deck and watch the eruption till its distant flames resembled the size and illumination of a hovering firefly.

The next morning Ted and I were in our bunks—asleep, when an ear-piercing sound forced our eyes open.

Buzzzzzzzzzz. Buzzzzzzzzz.

Dad jumped. Not hearing any directions coming over the speakers, he put his head out the door. "Anyone here know why the buzzer?"

The hallway was a mad house. People were pushing out of their doors, and over each other, all running for the top deck. Deciding that it was best to do likewise, Dad grabbed our four life jackets, quickly ushered us all out of the room and up the stairs.

On the way up Ted was told by one of the escapees that he had gone through a similar deal such as this only to discover it was a fire drill. But as we reached the main deck, the lifeboats were being let down. Just as Dad had once described, I watched wide-eyed as each one disappeared over the side of the ship. Down, down they traveled. *Kersplash!*

Now the rope ladders were unfurled. Many various workers on board started down the ropes.

"Oh, my goodness, look!" My hands quickly covered my mouth.

"Where?" Ted responded.

"Above, up there." Pointing to one of the rope ladders in the first section of the ship, it was crawling with the stewards in white uniforms.

"See him?"

"Whoa! Is that really him?" Ted questioned. He was trying to put the loose chords together. "Why isn't he in jail? The ship's jail?"

We watched him for as long as we could. He got off the ladder and into a life boat, where he directed the people handed to him. Then Aziz was gone, lost in the crowd.

That night, snuggled in his comfy berth, Ted had time to replay all of his *tamasha* on board. What an adventure.

From the shark episode to the Stromboli eruption –What had been the funniest? Scariest? The most thrilling? Some episodes had left lingering questions: Was the shark asleep or sick? And what about that little tin can? Will it ever see land? Will Aziz ever be caught?

As his eyes grew heavy, he once again heard a faint *buzzzzzzz.* Was it another fire drill? Or had the fireflies of slumber finally arrived to illuminate his dreams?

The day dawned bright and beautiful. As I was waking up the Empress of Russia was just pulling into the huge harbor of Marseilles, France. I sat up and rubbed my eyes. Looking out at today's world I saw many kinds of boats and ships–fishing boats, sightseeing boats, guiding boats, pilot boats–all competing for a place in the harbor. I'll just put off doing the regular morning chores for now, I decided. Looking out of the porthole was just too much fun.

"Hey, Ted, wake up! I wonder where that little boat is going—see the red one with the sail on top? And look at the one with a flat bottom. Right there. See it? Right beside our ship...Ted? Teddy? Ted Flaiz, Junior!!"

I was trying desperately to get Ted to see the exciting things that I was looking at. With my hand I was gesturing where the flat-bottomed boat was. "Wake up. Wake up, Ted."

Stirred by my insistent chatter, he finally stirred and sleepily opened his eyes and squinted out of the window.

"Waoh! Sis! Look! We've made it to France!"

For perhaps an hour we watched as our ship gently glided its way to the dock. With the help of various little guiding boats pulling and pushing, the massive vessel finally came to a stop.

It was now good-bye time for all of the boat friends from England, Germany, Scandinavia, and other parts of Europe. One more big ship and we would arrive at our final destination - America!

~ seven ~

A Funny Prank?

From our vantage point it seemed our mischief was to be taken more as a joke than as a crime.

By train we traversed France. After a fast skip across the English Channel, we reached our next port of call, Southampton. And there was our ship! Absolutely huge! The Europa.

"This is the biggest ship in the whole world," our steward told us as we were settling in to our cabin. We didn't like this one as much as we had liked the first one. This one was all so dressed up and fancy like. There was one special thing though that we really did appreciate about this ship-and that was a good-bye party that they were putting on the last night out. Everybody was invited. Ted and I were happy about that.

The dining room! It was absolutely beautiful! Silver and gold trusses, flowers, crystal goblets, soft lights, and bunches of balloons were dancing in the starlight. All of the grownups were dressed in evening gowns and tuxes. The orchestra was playing softy as the folks chose their chairs.

The balloons caught Ted's eye. When the workers were blowing them up just before the party started, Ted got up the courage to ask the lady if she had any extras. She was in a hurry and seemed happy to have a few less balloons to blow up. She gave Ted a bunch, and he stuffed them into his pockets.

In his crafty little head a plan was brewing.

It was night time. The party was over, and I was cuddled up with Ketchup in my upper berth. As I looked out of the porthole, all that I could see was the white foam of the splashing waves – splashing away from the side of the ship.

Huge waves. It was just too scary to look at I decided. What was Mom doing I wondered.

Looking below, the light was faint, from the transom.

"She's asleep," I said to Ketchup. "Dad and Ted, too.... Hey, with all of them asleep, I guess that I alone am master of my ship....master of my destiny."

I was getting carried away with my importance. But why not? With everyone now asleep, it was obvious that I was in charge of what was real, what was obvious.

"You see, Ketchup, when we get to America we will be back in your home place and you will be so happy again. But me? How can I ever be happy? No place but India will ever make me happy again." Brushing her hair, I continued.

"When we want to go for a look in the jungle, where will the elephants be? And how about Tommy Tucker? Who's going to see him to sleep at night? Then, of course, there's walking Coo a Coo. I know that he's so sad that we're not there. It's gonna be real bad trying to go to sleep without

the hyenas and the jackals howling. I dread thinking of all of the changes we will have to go through. . ."

***

The morning brought with it the promise of a great new day. America! It better be special like Mom has promised it will be. "Wake up, Honey. Wake up!" Mom was shaking me. "Look out of the window. We're just now going by the Statue of Liberty. Oh, this is so exciting. And look–look there is Manhattan."

I popped out of bed in an instant. I didn't want to miss a thing: Disembarking of the ship....catching of a taxi cab.... finding a hotel. And all kinds of other important things to do.

Everything was new to us kids. Elevators. Escalators. Telephones. And when we reached our room, on the 34th floor, I ran straight to the window to look out on the great city of New York.

"Is this really and truly the hugest, biggest city in the whole wide world?"

"It is," Dad answered. "But before we go any further we have to work out a plan to get out of New York as soon as possible. We have to be on the west coast in just over two weeks. Mom and I are going downtown to get a bunch of needed supplies for our trip. Who wants to go with us?"

"Sis and I don't want to go," Ted announced. "Think we'll just stay here and rest awhile." Emphasizing his claim, Ted plopped down on his bed, as though in a great need of rest.

"Hey, what's the big deal? Nobody asked me if I wanted to go," I spoke up.

A wink from Ted silenced my protest, but Dad was not so easily swayed.

"Okay, Mom and I will go get the supplies – but if we forget to get something for you, Ted, we don't want to hear anything about it later on. Understood?"

"Yeah, I hear ya," Ted mumbled.

"I didn't hear you, son."

"Okay! Alright! ...I promise."

The moment they were out the door, Ted jumped up and started pulling balloons from his pocket.

"Now, Sis, I want you to start filling these balloons with water. We're going to have some fun."

"So THIS was your crafty plan," I laughed. I was ready for anything.

"Get these balloons full," the Captain ordered with a grin, "we're going to toss them out of the window, out onto the street - thirty-four stories down. Hey, if they hit anybody they won't be hurt, just a little griped...and wet."

Such fun!

Captain Ted surmised that if we were real careful we could drop all the balloons without being detected. "If we toss one out every two or three minutes nobody will know where they're coming from."

Pretty soon there was a bunch of people below our window. Too far away to hear what was being said, but very evident that something was wrong.

"All right!" Ted sang out, rubbing his hands with glee. "We're drumming up a storm and nobody knows who's doing it."

Afraid of being detected we looked out of the window very briefly. And what we saw delighted us immensely: People scrambling for parts of balloons... People looking up at the side of the hotel...One woman running onto the street to grab her hat...And people telling each other what had happened to them.

From our vantage point it seemed our mischief was to be taken more as a joke than as a crime.

"This is getting down to your last balloon," I announced with fanfare. "Be sure it hits just right, 'cause you don't have many more chances."

Ted went to the window with this precious trophy. "Who shall I honor with one of my last balloons?" he pondered. Patiently he waited for just the right nominee.

"Ah ha, there she is!" And waiting for just...the...right moment, he let go. "Bombs away!"

This was no ribbon, or topi...it was a massive balloon, filled to the brim with tap water. And...BAMMM! The sortie exploded just in front of his victim.

Instantly the woman looked up. But seeing nothing but a skyscraper of windows, she kicked the balloon remnants out of her way, and walked on. Instead of having all of our fun at one time we decided to spread it out through the day into the afternoon.

Mom and Dad arrived back at our room 'bone' tired, but happy, and spread out on the bed the findings of the afternoon.

"How did the day go for you? Mom inquired. "Did you get all rested up from being soooo tired?" She had a sly knowing smile on her face.

Ketchup was asleep on my lap—a co-conspirator of the day's travails. And before I had a chance to answer, Mom spoke up again, "Just now, as we were downstairs at the desk, the clerk was in quite a state. She was talking to someone, and all that I could make of it was that there were folks coming in and complaining about getting wet out on the sidewalk. I think she said that balloons were falling from the sky?! That! Well it just doesn't make any sense."

"So?" Ted grunted, his head buried in a *National Geographic.*

"Well, I was just wondering if you kids might have heard anything about it," persisted Mom. Ted shrugged his shoulders. And I kept working on Ketchup's hair.

***

Again it was night time. It had been a fun – a happy day. A little wet at times, but still a good day.

Mom, Dad and Ted were fast asleep. But me? No, not yet. Too many things to sort out. Too many things to question, to place in the right perspective. In a short time we will be on our way across this new and awesome land. In the end how will it stand up to crossing India? Will the people be as friendly, as accepting? How about the jungles?

Will they be as lush and green as those of India? And how about the animals living here? Will they be at home in the wild, like the savage ones in India? I hope so. And then, of course, the snakes. I'm hoping that there won't be quite as... many......of.......

Sinking into slumber, I felt myself slip back home...back to the land my childhood knew....

~ eight ~

India

Arrivals & Returns

"Three years ago, on September 18th, at 5 o'clock in the morning, were you in any kind of trouble—you or your family?"

The date, September 8, entered the world as a clear and beautiful day. The mynah birds were scattering their songs in a triumph of being alive. The crows were endlessly scrapping with each other in an effort to prove that they were right. The canal drivers were in harness, pulling their crafts to the rhythm of the songs they sang. The world was in tune with itself and so it was that the little old man—the man who gave out prophesies according to the things that happened, said solemnly, "If it's Missy and she comes today she will be greatly blessed." And truly that is what happened.

Our family in Narsapur

The baby—when she came—was a delight to her family. Mom and Dad and little Teddy were in a joyous mood. A mood to welcome number four into the family. A mood to wish for mankind all of the blessings that life can afford. But beyond that, hope for God to bless this little bundle of joy. In the give and take of life, could He give to her the advantages of a dearly loved daughter? Thank you, God. We will trust you.

But in a few days it became evident that not all was well. On the third day Mother started to run a fever. She tried to shake it off, but no amount of effort could dissuade the heat from taking over her body. On the sixth day some cramping started to appear, and she had no fresh milk for the baby. No grocery store or dairy to alleviate the problem. What to do?

In pondering the situation Marthama, Mother's close-knit servant, suggested the possibility of buffalo milk. Oh, my goodness. Much too heavy. Too rich for a brand new baby. We can't use that. But when all of the possibilities were expended—there was nothing left to do. So Dad went to the bazaar and found some fresh buffalo milk. He bought it and brought it home. He let it sit for awhile, letting the cream rise to the top. He then took the remaining milk and cooked it. How was baby going to accept it? This was the big question, for in the answer lay the whole future of this baby. Was her tummy going to deal with this strange food, or was it going to turn away?

Dad watched the proceeding with bated breath. Will she? Won't she? Missy was very hungry sucking on the milk bottle, and Dad was delighted to see the familiarity with which she accepted the drink. With the emptying of the bottle she gave a half smile and settled down for a sleep. Dad tiptoed out of the room satisfied that all was well.

Every few minutes he would return to the room and barely, barely open the door. "All quiet," he would report to no one in particular. He was just thankful that all was quiet and peaceful.

As each day passed by, it became evident that Mother was losing ground. And it was this particular day that she came to the point that she could not communicate any longer. Not with Dad. Not with Marthama. Going from room to room, back and forth, Dad began to wonder just what his efforts were accomplishing. Not much, he decided, and in utter desperation he knelt down between rooms and poured out his heart to God. "Dear God, I've given it all I can. You'll have to take over now. I've given up everything for this move to India but without my wife and my child I just don't know how I can go on."

Suddenly he heard a cry. It was Missy.

Going to her room he saw that she had thrown up. Marthama had just beat him there and was already in the process of cleaning up the baby. When she had finished she said to Dad, "I have a friend who's baby was just like Missy. She couldn't drink buffalo milk so the wise man of the village told the mother to cook some chicken and give baby the broth. It worked real well. Maybe we should try it for Missy."

No sooner said than done, Dad had the broth all ready to go. Warm and tasty, he watched as Missy eagerly drank it down. This time when she finished the bottle she fell asleep. Dad felt more assured now that it would last. And so it did.

Missy took a long time to heal from her difficulty in eating, but as the weeks passed by it became evident that chicken broth was her savior. Mother on the other hand kept getting weaker and weaker, and she fell into a deep depression. It became evident that she had contracted puerperal fever. Dad tried to feed her and she was barely able to swallow. Then one day this rite came to an end and Dad realized that this was it. What more could he do? He

Marthama, Mother's close-knit servant

went out on the back porch of the house and sat down to think things through again. Again for the tenth, no fifteenth --or was it the twentieth time? He couldn't remember. He seemed numb with discouragement. No doctors within hundreds of miles. No phone to call a doctor.

The back side of the house edged on the play yard of the school. This was the mission school that he had started just two years before. This is why he had come to India—to accomplish this mission. And now only to leave my most precious possession —my Jennie—in the ground of this far off land. "I can't, God. I just can't go on."

The school bell rang and out of the building streamed the children—full of life and energy ready for recess. As Dad watched them in their lively play it suddenly dawned on him the amount of prayer power that was resident in the group. Hadn't many of them already told him how much they wanted Memshab to get well and how they were praying for her?

Dad walked over and whistled them to a stop. "School will be over in just two hours," he said. "Those of you who would like to join me in praying for Memshab, come by and we will all pray for her together."

For two hours Dad sat by Jennie holding her hand. He noted her breathing and her general condition. It was deteriorating rapidly. He had heard of Chain stokes respiration as being the final performance of a person with a condition such as this, never believing that it would hit him at such a time. Her breaths came slowly—ever so slowly, and one was left to wonder if another would be coming in time. As Dad awaited the arrival of the children he became desperate wondering whether or not Mom would draw the next breath. He prayed that Jennie would indeed hold on to life until that time.

Soon he became aware that the group was forming. They were coming from every side. Not only children but moms and dads, teachers and just plain friends. Dad had them sit on the ground all around him. He opened his Bible to the various promises therein and read them with the utmost devotion. He then invited each one who wished to—to take part in prayer. Many were the anguished requests made to God that afternoon. When the last one had made his requests, Dad thanked them each one for coming and for taking part in the occasion.

He then went into the house daring to see if Mother was still alive. And to his surprise he saw a fresh looking girl with a half smile on her face. She was sound asleep and breathing normally. Dad knelt down beside her, took her hand, and thanked God for the great change he saw in her. In two hours she opened her eyes and asked for some food. What a joy! Thank you. Thank you, heavenly Father. I'll never question your ways again. Believe me.

Mother's healing was like a shot-in-the-arm to the whole community – like nothing before. Many villagers came to see the woman that the great spirit of the cosmos had healed—had healed at the request of the children of the school and of course it gave to the Christian man—their leader—a certain sanctity to be so closely associated to the center of power. It also gave considerable meaning to the school and to what it stood for, which nothing could discount.

The addendum to this episode of arrivals and returns took place three years later, during a family furlough in

America. After a meeting in Montana, where Dad had just given a talk on India, he was standing in the church doorway bidding good-bye to the parishioners, when a lady he had never met clasped his hand. The woman offered him a friendly smile. She paused, then finally spoke.

"I have a question to ask of you—one that means a lot to me."

"Yes?"

Opening her purse, she retrieved a little scrub of paper.

"Ah, here it is! Three years ago, on September 18th, at 5 o'clock in the morning were you in any kind of trouble—you or your family?"

Dad paused and started thinking back. Soon a conscious recognition crossed his face. *Could it be? Could it really be?*

"Why do you ask?" he questioned.

"Well, a number of years ago I was reading the current church paper, and I came across a picture of you and your wife leaving for India. You both looked so young, and I determined that you would have a great many trials and tribulations to endure. I knew you needed considerable prayer. You have been on my prayer list ever since.

Pausing to gather her thoughts, she glanced at the date scribbled on the paper. "It was five o'clock on that morning that I was awakened with a strong impression that you folks needed prayer. It was a little early, but I got out of bed and went for my morning walk. In a few moments I stopped and knelt, and called your names out to God. When finished I felt that I should keep a note of the day and hour of this experience, just in case I ever had the opportunity some day of meeting you. "

As Dad listened to her story, he had figured the timing and realized that this was indeed not just the day, but the self same hour that the children had joined him and, "*yes.*" It was an answer of faith for my father, mother and the lady with the question.

Ted and Jennie Flaiz, my parents, on their wedding day

September 3, 1918

~ *nine* ~

An Exotic Land

English was a foreign sound to us.

As the days and months passed by, Dad and Mom realized that they were still in the process of getting used to this fabulous land called India. They found that India is protected from any army advancing from the north by the tiers of mountains known as the Himalayas.

From the east they were protected by the Bay of Bengal, from the south—the Indian Ocean, and by the west—the Arabian Sea. From the immense mountains of the north with their craggy lofts and ice covered snow fields to the huge rivers that crisscross the land to the south—all of the country seemed to possess an intensity and awareness that could not be ignored.

The earliest evidence of civilization comes from the buried cities of the Sind area—northwestern India. When dug out these cities present well planned buildings and homes. Probably the earliest recordings of this era would be that of Alexander the Great pushing his army into India right up to the banks of the Indus River. This was some three hundred years before the birth of Christ.

My folks found a productively rich land populated by 338,000,000 very, very poor people.

For transportation they found very few cars, but many, many camels, bicycles, rickshaws, bullock carts, motorcycles, and many trains that the British had provided. These rails cover practically all of India—but mostly hover around the large cities.

There were far reaching jungles populated by the tiger (The Royal Bengal Tiger is the symbol of India), many varieties of bear, leopard, elephants, monkeys, hyenas, and deer. They were the most numerous of the wild animal types.

My parents were stationed in the southern part of the country–the less inhabited area of land. They found that the rivers which cross the country bring to that land the needed water to feed the crops of wheat and rice. In the month of May the winds start blowing in the southern part of the Indian Ocean. As they come north they begin to build. When these movements of rain begin to hit the mountains, they break apart, dumping huge amounts of water thus forming the headquarters of these rivers.

These movements of water are called the monsoons. Not only do they flush out the grubbiness of the forest, but they present a freshness to the whole jungle–both in scent, sight and taste.

And what about politics?

Well, it seems that the majority of Indians at that time embraced the Hindu (Congess) party, next the Muslim party, and then a tiny few took up the Communist line holding to this situation indefinitely. Overlooking the land, the British decided that the Hindus and Moslems needed to be separated –thereby quelling the tide of continual fighting. It was decided to give the western and northeastern area to the Moslems, calling it Pakistan and Bangladesh and leaving the entire middle and eastern section for the Hindus.

Looking at a map one can see that from north to south it is approximately 2,000 miles and taking another look one can see that it is about the same going from east to west.

The language is complicated and frankly—quite a hassle. It is a totally different alphabet and figures. Dad and Mom were amazed to hear that they were given a whole year to work on their language study. They have always been thankful for the gift of that one year. It left them well positioned to care for any occasion that might arise. We

The way we loved to ride

children grew up with only the language of Telegue being heard. English was a foreign sound to us.

It is estimated that there are 1,652 dialects in India, this situation being a problem for the education of the whole country. At that time the population of the country was 15%

literate. That along with being one of the poorest countries of the world gave to India the distinction of being a country in great need..

The village of Narsapur is a small fishing village on the banks of the Bay of Bengal. Dad and Mother had their positions cut out for them—a school primarily and an emergency room coming later on. In speaking to many of the "knowing" folks it was a given that a school would be the magnet to start a mission station. Education was at such a high premium that they could already envision a thriving school in progress. However they were soon to learn that finances trumped the lot.

Try as they might the going in their early days in Narsapur was slow – mighty slow. Perhaps if I tell you a couple of stories in the next two chapters of their early days in Narsapur it would help to settle the playing field.

So here goes–.

~ ten ~

Choir in the Jungle

Whenever the path grew heavy with doubt,
one mention of that special night, and
the heaviness would soon be gone.

From her vantage point beneath the banyon tree Jennie watched as twilight crept silently across the Indian plains. In the distance a pale half moon began its slow climb into the night sky, silhouetting a clump of waving palm trees.

It was the moment when the rulers of the day give way to those of the night. For at dusk one can hear the day–end blatting of the goats, the mooing of the buffalo, and the chattering of the baboons in the tree tops. Twenty two year old Jennie knew well the scenario as she had witnessed it on many occasions. She awaited now the first howl of the jackal and the grunts of the wild boar digging in the peanut field next to the tent. Then there would surely come the screams of the night hawk searching for its supper and the whirr of the bats as they escaped their daytime hiding places.

Mysterious, magical, haunting: It was night time in the Indian jungle.

As the forest symphony accelerated, Jennie moved her camp chair closer to the tent where her two babies –the new baby girl, Junie, and two year old Teddie lay fast asleep.

Just above her hung a kerosene lantern tied loosely to a branch of the banyon tree. As it swayed gently in the evening breeze it lit up the campsite and cast dancing shadows on the side of the tent. A short distance away she could see and hear her husband, Ted, tell with animated voice the story of Jesus to the village people. Light from the flickering campfire reflected on their up turned faces. It thrilled her to see how the large Picture Roll stimulated an interest in the stories of the Bible.

But lately things seemed different. There was no thrill. No excitement. It had been a long day, a hot day. Discouragement often follows in the wake of tiredness, and on this night Jennie was truly tired.

There had been two little ones to attend to, little ones who rebelled at the flies, the dust, the heat. Their care had competed with the care of the sick villagers who stood in line sometimes for hours, awaiting advice and medicine. And Jennie had not neglected the major reason for this trip—that of developing recruits for the kingdom of heaven.

The enemy of Christianity had for centuries—yes, millennia—held these people captive to vengeful gods made of wood and stone. And now as Ted and Jennie, through Picture Rolls and Bible Stories, portrayed a God of love some of the villagers were moved, yes, thrilled by the news. But most were afraid to take a stand, for fear of the threats made by the heathen priests.

The challenges of developing a mission school and churches within a culture so deeply ingrained in its own Hindu religion at times seemed overwhelming. In frustration Jennie began a one-sided dialogue with God.

"I am so homesick tonight, dear God. Really homesick. Sometimes I wonder if we're accomplishing anything out here— anything at all. For months now we've been waiting for more help with the school. More help in finances and for more help in personnel. And today it seemed like so many things went wrong. We ran out of medicine just when we needed it most. Then there were the two flat tires on the car when we drove to the next village. It took hours to fix them.

I'm sorry to be discouraged, Lord, but I'm wondering if we really truly are accomplishing anything for you."

Just then a familiar voice broke through her reverie. "Discouraged, honey?" Ted asked diagnosing well the present situation. "It seems like we've had more than enough challenges lately." He paused momentarily, searching for a veneer to cover his own disappointments. "We mustn't forget that another day is coming, Jennie. The Lord will open up a way."

He hoped that his voice sounded cheery, hopeful.

It was late, time to break camp.

With home as a goal, time sped by quickly. The tent came down. It was folded and packed into the old convertible touring car. Next followed sleeping cots, utensils, bedding, and last the babies, carefully tucked into the back seat, sound asleep.

The "road" home was really a bullock cart trail, bumpy and pockmarked. Herds of water buffalo had long plied this trail, leaving their signature foot prints in the muddy ruts.

Ted's full attention was focused on driving, while Jennie continued to ponder the challenges of the day. Just then a beautiful holy sound penetrated their senses.

"Oh, Ted. Stop....listen." The old car ground to a halt.

"What is it, Ted. What is it?"

"It can't be a radio," he answered with mounting excitement. "No radios in this part of India. Besides we're miles from any village."

They spoke in hushed reverent tones.

"It isn't Indian music so... it can't be something... local."

It took a moment but two amazed listeners realized that the music was filtering down...from the sky directly above them.

The melody and words combined to create the most perfect harmony they had ever heard. In stunned silence they sat transfixed. Could this be possible?

For fifteen minutes a heavenly choir serenaded them, wrapping them in an aura of peace and tranquility. As they listened, many were the thoughts that flooded their minds. Among those thoughts, there was a realization that the God of heaven was aware of them, individually, aware of the many problems of the past few months. And that He wished to encourage them by sending a choir of angels to serenade them, and show them his love and care.

In that atmosphere, disappointments became challenges. Doubts turned into possibilities. With God as their partner, how could they become discouraged? How could they give up?

Slowly, ever so slowly the music began to fade into the sky above them. In an effort to hold onto this precious moment they strained to catch every note. When silence finally reigned once again, Ted and Jennie bowed their heads in grateful thanks for the wondrous gift that had blessed their lives that day.

The memory of that special night never grew dim. Whenever the path grew heavy with doubt, one mention of that special night, and the heaviness would soon be gone.

This again isn't the end of the story.

Through the years the Narsapor school reports have been thrilling to receive. However a recent report capped them all. Suvarna Raj, principal of the school, sent this e-mail message:

Greetings from Flaiz Memorial Seventh-Day Adventist College. Are you astonished by my opening remarks? Our Naraspur Mission School has become a full-fledged college approved by the Indian government and affiliated with the University of Andhra Pradesh.

As I read the message, my mind slipped back to the long ago, to a night forever blessed by God's stepping into my parents' dimension for 15 minutes, bringing a message of love, encouragement, and hope to two tired and discouraged young people.

~ eleven ~

Thinking Outside the Box

"Our gods will direct Mauri ... and he will be ours...
No more Christian school.
No more Christian god."

It was a rainy monsoon morning. Mom was busy in the kitchen baking some bread. In a moment Dad walked by. "Say, Hon," Mom called, "I just saw Mauri and his dad. It looked like they were arguing out on the school compound. Can't imagine what about."

"Think maybe I'd better drop by and see."

Dad rerouted his steps toward the school compound.

Mauri was ten years old and in the fourth grade. He was a sweet and happy boy—putting all of his extra energy into helping others—both students and teachers alike. So it came as a surprise one day to see him arguing with his dad on the school compound.

"No. I won't go," he said dismissively to his father. "I'm staying right here."

Dad wondered what the fuss was about and stepped in.

"What's the problem, Mauri? Anything that I can help you with?"

It was school time and Marui was out of his room. With a heavy frown on his face and the arguing ongoing, Dad turned to the father.

"Perhaps you could help me out, Riju. Could you explain what Mauri's problem is?"

Now Riju was a simple farmer—a rice farmer —and he loved his boy very much. He was happy to have two boys and when a school opened in Narsapur—just three miles away from his village— he felt greatly blessed. The gods had been good. He was delighted that Marui—instead of working in the rice fields every day—was in school learning—learning about that big old world out there. The work load was much higher for him, now, but it was totally worth every bit of the cost.

Some time before, when Marui registered for school, his father was the happiest man in the crowd. He was beaming from ear to ear. Dad had noticed him and remembered him—thinking highly of him.

Now the story was changing.

"It's the high priest," said Riju, his eyes flashing. "He tells me and the village that Mauri has to come home. The gods have changed their minds. He says that they will curse our rice harvest and destroy it if he doesn't come back to the village and get away from these Christians and their god. And many, many other bad things will happen."

"And do you believe him, Riju?"

"I have to believe him. He's my priest."

"I don't believe him!" said Mauri. "And I will pray to God to not let anything happen to our rice crop. You'll see!" Mauri declared this with all of the emphasis a ten year can display.

Dad saw a huge problem developing and tried to waylay it for now. "It is almost test time now, Riju, and we will go into the problem when the time comes."

This answer seemed to placate Riju for now, so nodding goodbye to Mauri, he turned and started back home. The rain was now coming down in torrents so Dad asked if he wouldn't like to stay at the school until it let up a bit.

"No. No," Riju pointed down the road, "I have much work to do." So with his ever-present walking stick in hand, he started down the now muddy path. Dad with his tender heart felt badly over his decision as he watched him disappear into the mists of the monsoon.

My parents saw little Mauri from time to time but never brought up the subject of his leaving. Too painful. Where as if left alone, hopefully it would melt away.

Time slipped by and then one day they heard a noise—a ruckus—coming from down the canal bank. What could it be? The closer it came the more concerned the school people became.

Finally they broke out from behind the trees along the canal. Rows and rows of villagers were banging on all kinds of paraphernalia. At the front were their Hindu priest and Riju —looking most uncomfortable.

On they came. Right up to the school entrance. When the priest put up his hands to stop the crowd and the noise, Dad was there to greet them.

"Hello," said Dad with a smile. "Saleem. Saleem. Can I help you?"

"Shhh. Shhh," the priest demanded, trying to subdue the crowd. "We've come to get Mauri. To take him home. "

"I'm not sure that Mauri is ready to leave the school yet," answered Dad.

"In that case," the priest huffed, "we have planned a meeting. It will be in five more nights. You bring Mauri to our village. We will have a big box on poles to carry him. At the meeting we will pray to the gods that Mauri will get into the box when we start the music."

Some of the villagers were getting restless. It had been a long walk from their village. The priest banged his walking stick on the ground and shouted at the crowd to shape up. "Our gods will direct Mauri to get into the box and he will be ours from then on. No more Christian school. No more Christian god." The priest, pointing his walking stick directly at Dad, added, "Tell me, Thogorado, will you be there? And will you bring Mauri?"

"We surely will be there," Dad answered, "and we thank you for coming today."

With that they all picked up their noise makers and left the school.

By now all of the students were wondering. What was all the *tamasha* about? So many people. So much banging. Hanging out of the classroom windows they were trying to catch a sentence of explanation.

Stepping inside Dad asked Mauri to join him in front of the room. Putting his arm around Mauri, he asked all to bow their heads.

"Dear Jesus, Mauri has been with us for a long time now, and we appreciate him very much. He has been such a good boy, and we don't want to lose him. Please be with him and keep him from getting into that box. Thank you. Amen."

Dad was surprised to hear another voice going up to God for help, another then another. He then heard Mauri's voice repeating the same urgent request.

After Dad explained the problem to the children, he asked, "How many of you boys and girls would like to have a special prayer every day until Friday? And then go down to Mauri's village to this big meeting. Would you like to go down there?"

Every hand went up both for the prayer and for being present at the meeting.

It was a tense week. The box and the coming meeting were the subject of everyone's discussion during that week. Friday finally arrived and all were ready for the occasion. With so many of the students joining the group, there were many parents and family members wanting to go as well.

Before leaving the school Dad had prayer with the group sincerely asking God to show visibly his love and care.

Arriving at Mauri's village, my parents were amazed by the crowd. A huge fire was burning right in the middle of the village. Children were sitting around it, with the adults encircling them.

And there - in front of the whole group - was the box and the four men who were to carry it. Chairs were quickly gathered about and placed by the box. The priest seemed to be directing everything. He had a chair for Mauri, for Dad and Mom, and the school's teacher, Mr. Davidoss.

When things quieted down a bit and the villagers were seated – on the ground – the four men stood and picked up the box. The priest explained that the men would carry it around the fire and then when they reached Mauri, they would put it down for Mauri to step into. It then would be carried off somewhere. He didn't explain to where.

It was then that the "music" started with a bang, and I do mean *bang*. All kinds of noise makers–even detached car horns joined the crowd. The box carriers started a dance as they moved around the circle, yelling and crying to their gods to make Mauri jump into the box.

Mauri had his head bowed and was praying as the men brought the box to him. They dropped the box in front of him and stood back to watch him slip into it. They waited and waited but nothing happened. Nothing happened except that the noise increased to a frenzy.

Angrily they got up and with more vigor carried the box around again. They called out to their gods demanding to have Mauri jump into the box. Still nothing took place.

The Christian children all were praying.

Again and again they took the box around, as the priest pleaded his case. "Please - please, oh gods, show us your strength!"

The surroundings reminded Dad of the scene from the Bible, when the four hundred priests of Baal pleaded with their god, while Elijah stood by watching.

Finally the box was placed in front of Mauri again. Everyone waited and prayed.

Then out of nowhere, a man on his hands and knees crawled out of the crowd and slipped into the box. The men picked him up and carried him out into the utter darkness of the night.

What happened to him, we never found out.

"Thank you, thank you, God," Dad offered in great appreciation for His care during that day.

And as for Mauri, I am glad to say, that he continued to think outside the box of the superstitious past, and held to his Christianity throughout his long life.

~ twelve ~

Abraham & the Rajah

" ...the Lord sometimes uses strange and unusual characters in the development of His plans."

After starting the school in Nasapur Dad felt that he needed some men who knew something about the Gospel and who were true to what they knew. There were a few such men in the city of Bezwada perhaps eight or ten whom he contacted.

"Would you be interested in selling literature to the people of the Narsapur area?" he asked them. "Your efforts would develop an interest in both the Gospel and among the people to send their children to our school."

He was thrilled with the response. In those first two years of the mission development there were a good number of young men and not so young men who applied for positions as teachers and evangelists. These volunteers would be required to first undergo one year of successful book selling. And of these applicants Dad invited the most promising to the Colporteur Institute, an organization devoted to the art of selling Bible storybooks.

Among those who were accepted was a man named Parti Abraham. He was obviously a man of wide experience and ability. Yet there was something about him that led one to exercise more than usual caution in placing trust in him.

Another prospect who came to this first Colporteur meeting was a fine young cheerful fellow by the name of Samuel. About the second morning of their meeting Samuel made a humorous remark toward Parti Abraham.

"Parti, you look just like an old grandma in your shawl this morning." The remark was so appropriate, so accurately

descriptive of Parti that everyone enjoyed a good laugh. However Abraham's reaction was not so jovial. Hearing the laughter Parti flew into a rage and attacked Samuel with a rather wide vocabulary of Telegue profanity and curses.

Immediately Dad took Parti by the arm and led him outside. He explained to the man that he was "done" and told him to return at noon when he would be given back his fare to Bezwada.

At noon a very humble Parti returned, begging to be taken back. The response was "Out of the question!" Relenting, the penitent man asked only that he be allowed to stay on for two more days and secure a ride with Dad upon his scheduled return to Bezwada – thus saving the price of the fare. Dad consented.

On the return ride, Parti mentioned to Dad that he had a good friend in that area, the Rajah of Teleprole. In India a Rajah was a glamorous, powerful ruler – his wishes were carried out, his authority never questioned. Until the British came, they were the rulers of India. When the English saw the reverence with which these rulers were treated, they simply took the top rung of power, and allowed the Rajahs to continue their regional control, providing a calming effect and a continuity of government.

Parti was quite sure that the Rajah would be glad to give Dad not only help for the schools of the area but whatever assistance he might need.

Though somewhat wary of Abraham, his offer of an introduction to such an influential figure piqued Dad's interest. So, he altered the route of his trip to hazard a visit with the Rajah.

On the way Parti had reached into his pocket and pulled out a fine Venus pencil—very popular in India at that time. Holding it up for Dad to see he boasted, "This is what the Rajah gave me when I last visited him."

There was something not quite right in the man's smile. But later that evening, to Dad's delight, Abraham managed to obtain an invitation to meet the Rajah at nine o'clock the following morning.

Arriving at the then beautifully kept palace grounds they were taken to a court where the Rajah was overseeing some work. He was most cordial, accepting Dad's school papers with obvious interest. He was about to hand them back when he saw a note on the back page – a note about the medical work we were now doing in northern India.

He was immediately interested.

Becoming quite intimate and introspective, the Rajah revealed that in about 1908 his mother was overtaken with a serious illness. His father, in his great concern, took a solemn vow that if one of the gods would restore his mother to health again he would build a hospital in Nuzvid for the women of the city.

The mother recovered. Two or three years later the father died. This left the son—now the new Rajah of Teleprole—as the one responsible for the fulfillment of the vow. And so it was that in 1913 the Rajah started to build the hospital.

There was good progress on the building for a few months until the war in Europe erupted in July of 1914. All of the building supplies were then taken for the war effort in Europe. The building of the hospital was brought to an abrupt halt.

Now eight years later, the Rajah invited Dad to go over to the hospital site to see what had been done. Arriving at the gate there was only a break in the cactus hedge—some old

The Rajah and Rani

broken down wooden posts with some strands of barbed wire across to keep the buffaloes out.

After showing Dad around this bush grown property the Rajah said that if he would take over the hospital and develop it as a good general hospital he would deed it over and give Dad 10,000 Rupee – his first contribution. Naturally Dad accepted the offer- awaiting confirmation from the General Conference of Seventh-day Adventist Church in America. It came in late 1923, and the building began immediately.

Just a further word concerning Parti Abraham. When he learned that because of his mention to the Rajah we were now building a fine hospital, he felt that there should be some kind of reward for him. He renewed his request for employment. Dad was sure that he was not fit for regular mission work but it occurred to him that with thousands of rupees worth of teak boards in our carpentry shed we needed a watchman. And so it was that Dad decided to try him out.

During that year of building Dad was carrying the load of the Narsapur mission along with the hospital. He would work all day, then leave in the car for Nuzvid in the late evening, arriving there in the early morning—at three or four o'clock.

One time when there were rather large stacks of teak boards standing on the veranda where Parti lived (as our faithful watchman), Dad arrived expecting to find his night watchman on guard. But there was no one there but a large, valuable stack of exposed teak boards.

Taking his flashlight Dad went around to Abraham's quarters and found the man sound asleep by his lantern on the porch. Seeing another small stack of teak nearby, Dad walked over and cautiously tipped it back until it came crashing to the floor. In a flash Parti jumped to his feet, grabbed his lantern, dashed inside, and locked the door.

Shaking his head, Dad returned to his car and slept in the back seat until daylight when he was greeted by his cheerful watchman. With that same smile Parti then reported how he had bravely guarded the property from a robber who had come during the night.

Poor man. When Abraham found out that the robber was actually his employer, the man who loved the sound of his own voice was instantly silenced.

Front row: Punkie, Ted, Freddie and me
Back row: Dr. Coyne, Mom, Dr. Hughes, Mrs.Coyne and Dad

The completed hospital in Nuzvid

***

Later, writing of this experience, Dad mused, "I mention this failed colporteur, failed watchman, only to show how the Lord sometimes uses strange and unusual characters in the development of His plans. If He could use a Parti Abraham for so significant a purpose as to lead us to our first contact in Nuzvid, there is a place for everyone who is truly dedicated to the service of the Lord."

~ thirteen ~

Christmas in America

"If you could have anything in this whole wide world that you really, really wanted for Christmas," Cousin Harriet asked... *"What would you choose?"*

It was decided that our family should take the coming year as our twelve month furlough. And upon our return, we would move to Nuzvid. Dad would oversee the hospital and also the mission activities, and a man would come to take over the immediate duties of the Narsapur school seventy-five miles away.

On that pre-arranged day, Ted and I had to say good-bye to our dear friends-the kids of the mission. And with a snap of the fingers, we went from the world of Telegue, to the world of English.

It was a big change.

Arriving in Walla Walla, Washington, was indeed a big day. Grandpas, grandmas, uncles, aunties, and cousins were all there to greet us. By now Ted and I had garnered a bit of English in our vocabulary and we would mix it up with Telegue. Our cousins loved to listen to our mix-up and always have a good laugh. Being a shy and reticent child, I took their amusement as a negative and often cried. But eventually things settled down and our cousins took the place of our little friends in Narsapur.

We made our home with our paternal grandpa and grandma in the town of College Place, Washington. They lived in a house just across the street from Walla Walla College.

"...It's just too good a chance to learn something," Dad soon realized, pointing to the campus just outside the living room window. And with my Mom in tow, they both enrolled in college. Given that endeavor, along with speaking engagements all over the northwest, the two quickly became a very busy couple.

Living next door to grandpa and grandma was Uncle Ross, my dad's older brother. Ross and his wife, Eleanor, had two little girls – Harriet and Betty. The girls were a little bit older than Ted and I—by three or four years, and were very proper and correct in all that they said and did. Ted and I continually bugged them, and their responses were always charitable.

We were considered an interesting but strange couple of kids to observe. We couldn't speak English, and all we wanted to eat was rice and curry, and that really hot. Where was Marthama when I needed her? How about the songs of the canal? I missed those lullabies at bedtime. And where was Ago, our goat who ate up half of my mosquito netting one night?

These were the problems that affected me and since I couldn't do anything about them I would cry myself to sleep many a night.

The holidays were coming, and my parents were convinced that Ted and I should be introduced to a real Christmas. And so it was that when Aunt Eleanor told Mom of her plans for the day, Mom was delighted.

"If you could have anything in this whole wide world that you really, really wanted for Christmas," Cousin Harriet asked, as if on a mission, "what would you choose?"

She had come over to deliver some fresh cookies her mom had just made. My Mom, standing close by, interpreted what I couldn't understand.

"What I want more than anything else in this whole world is...a doll.
One that has hair...and one that has eyes that move."

"I am hoping that Santa Claus will bring one down the chimney when he comes." In my mixed up Telegue/English I added, "And I hope that she will be wearing a pink dress and silver shoes."

Harriet was taking in all of the specifications and when I had finished she was gone.

Christmas dawned bright and sunny, and while the grownups were busy with Christmas goings–on, we children played Eskimo. We built an ice house – an igloo with a little rug inside and a box that looked like a stove. We asked Aunt Eleanor for different things that would make our mound of snow seem like a real house, and with cheerful cooperation she provided!

Finally it was evening and time to depart for supper—just next door. My goodness how beautiful it all was. Christmas music was on the Victrola, lights low, and supper smelled delicious.

The living room was adorned with a beautiful tree, all fixed up with lights and lovely decorations—stars, trumpets, angels—just waiting for Santa to appear and scatter the presents.

In the decorated dining room Aunt Eleanor had placed names on each plate, and we all circled the table finding our seat. The food was amazing, but I ate as fast as I could, cause I just couldn't wait for the next phase—Santa...and the presents!

Just as we were finishing dessert I heard some bells tinkling. I was too shy to say anything. The sound was coming from outside, and it was getting louder and louder. Finally someone picked up on it and cried out, "Does anyone hear the...reindeer? It's coming from....Outside!"

Aunt Eleanor got up and told all of us not to go outside - but to come into the living room and sit down.

I was so excited I could hardly breathe.

I found a chair beside the Christmas tree and sat down. The other folks found their places, and we all sat breathless awaiting Santa's arrival. The music came louder and louder. Pretty soon we heard - "*Ho. Ho. Ho.*"

Ted and Junie playing house in the snow

There was a knock on the door and Aunt Eleanor exclaimed, "It must be Santa." The door swung open and... sure enough, there he was! And over his shoulder was a huge pillow case full of packages!

"Good evening, boys and girls. And of course, Mommies and Daddies too. When I left the North Pole this morning it was sooooo cold but you know what? All of my friends the penguins, the polar bears, and reindeer were out to wish me well. And they–every one of them told me to be sure and give you their love." With that he put down his load and started pulling out the packages, one at a time.

Ted and Junie - *Brrrr* - it's cold!

"Oh I hope–I hope he remembers my doll..." I whispered, holding my hands together praying.

"Theodore–this one is for you," said Santa, as he passed the first present on to Ted.

And then came cousin Betty, and others, and finally he held up a package about the size of a really truly doll.

"Mary June. Is Mary June here?"

I was so shy I held back as Ted retrieved it for me.

All held still as I opened the package and there, lying in the box was the most beautiful doll that I had ever seen. Long golden blond hair, big blue eyes that opened and closed! I took her out of the box and held her tight, cradling her in my arms.

"Thank you Santa, thank you soooooo much."

"You're welcome, Mary June. Just one question though. I'm wondering what her name will be." Having forgotten all of my insecurities for the moment I was able to tell Santa right off: "...Ketchup."

"Ketchup?" a collection of voices all inquired. "Why Ketchup?"

There was a hint of twitter in the room. Somehow in my mixed up languages I explained that of all the new foods I had found in America, Ketchup was by far my favorite. And so it was that Ketchup became the fifth member of our family.

The months sped by and it was soon time to say good-bye again. This time it was to the extended family that we had learned to love.

We would be returning to my home though things would be a little bit different. For this time we would be living in Nuzvid—seventy-five miles from our old home in Narsapur.

When Ted or I would complain about the change, Dad would quiet us with a little bribe. "The Rajah has a bunch of elephants in Nuzvid. If we move there he will be so happy that he'll send his drivers over to take you kids for rides."

Riding elephants? It wasn't as good as Christmas, but it would do.

Going home to India - Ted and June

Our family heading back to India

~ fourteen ~

Haunted House

Closer, closer it came.
And then when the noise was right in front of him
Dad jumped at the sound and turned on the flash light.
Nothing. Absolutely nothing.

What a joy it was to see the heavily trafficked roads of India again. Not with cars, but with buffaloes, camels, rickshaws and bicycles. We were welcomed home by an enthusiastic crowd of workers from the school and from a small "hospital" that had been started in Narsapur during our absence. I use the word "hospital" rather loosely, for it was more like a clinic in America taking on all emergencies. To run this hospital the General Conference had recruited Dr. Coyne, his wife, a Registered Nurse and their two children.

Freddie and Punkie were the exact same ages as Ted and I. It was a miracle. Just to think that way out in India in a small rural village that four kids from America found each other.

Four little waifs: Junie, Ted, Freddie and Punkie

In Narsapur we packed up our household effects and drove to Nuzvid. Staying in the British made traveler's bungalow, located just outside of Nuzvid, we started looking for possible living sites. The hospital there was almost finished, and the Rajah was quite relived to see Dad and Dr. Coyne. He was relieved in the sense that he had someone now who could answer questions that he felt unable to do.

It was decided by the Rajah that he would build two nice homes very near to the hospital. One would be for the doctor in charge—the other for my Dad and his family. But until that time should arrive we would need a temporary shelter of some kind.

The Rajah remembered that he had an empty home right by the hospital sight. Dad asked him, "Why is the home empty?"

The answer was a little unsettling.

"Well...," he rubbed his head trying to put together an explanation. "You see," he continued, "this house has a reputation in the village of being...haunted. Strange things happen there, so everyone is afraid, not only to live there but to even walk by the place."

Dad's curiosity was stoked. "When did this start?"

"A number of years ago a Hindu priest cast a spell on the house."

"Sounds interesting," said Dad. "We'll take it."

And with that the Rajah sent over two servants to help with the settling-in process.

This house was known as the "Green Bungalow"—a rather pretty house surrounded by a high wall. One could imagine that the originator of the house was a flower lover, for the yard was strewn with many plants that had died long ago, leaving just a few barely surviving on the fringe.

That first day we got pretty well settled—all of the major parts stashed where they belonged. I noted that our four army cots were arranged on the side veranda, and I was curious as to why we weren't going to sleep in one of the side rooms, which we would call a bedroom.

Dad sat me down and caught Ted as he was running by. "I need to explain something to you kiddies." We sat down on a cot beside him. "The strange things that are going on at this house are nothing but the local folks who don't want a Christian to come to Nuzvid. These are the Hindu priests and such who are afraid that the influence of a Christian will take away their right over the people, and spoil it all for them."

"Will it?" Ted wondered.

"No, of course not, Buddy. But then if it did, might it be good? What do you think?"

Dad left us with that last question to mull over. How, we wondered, could a Christian mess things up for a Hindu? We decided to let Dad deal with it.

***

That night all was quiet as we fell asleep. But it wasn't to last. In a few moments Dad was awakened by the crashing of metal. It started up at the front section of the house. Going down the full length of the house was a hallway consisting of a rock flooring which resounded the noise in good fashion.

Quickly Dad jumped out of his mosquito netting, grabbed his flashlight and slipped into the back room of the house. There he positioned himself to pounce upon the man who was dragging those metals down the hall.

"I'll show him that he can't scare us out of Nuzvid," said Dad to himself.

Down the hall came the crashing, the banging–slowly, slowly.

"When he gets here I'll just jump out with the flashlight and give him a scare that he'll never forget!"

Closer, closer it came. And then when the noise was right in front of him Dad jumped at the sound and turned on the flash light.

Nothing. Absolutely nothing. No man. No metals to make the sound. Just nothing! Dad realized then that this was something completely beyond him, framed in the masterminds of the occult.

When he came back to bed–to the army cots that he and mother used when in temporary transmission, they discussed their plight. Should they just pick up and leave the Green Bungalow, or should they stick it out—and ask God for help through whatever they had to face.

Together they had prayer and decided that plan number two would be the one that they would follow.

~ fifteen ~

"It's that occult thing."

The low growl continued and escalated slowly into what was eventually a high pitched scream, higher and higher.

The Rajah soon heard all about the night of the banging and had a careful talk with one of his servants. With the American family there he was quite sure that such would not happen again.

The servant presented himself about bedtime along with a bedroll and a lantern. He explained that the Rajah had sent him over to be a guard for the night. He settled himself on the veranda, on the opposite side of the house, and was soon fast asleep.

Likewise our family, having put in a full and hectic day, was also fast asleep. Along about 2 A.M. there was a shrill cry that pierced the night air. *Who? What? Where?*

In a moment Dad was wide awake. *The servant!*

The screaming continued – piercing and shrill. Grabbing his ever-present flashlight, he bounded out of the mosquito net and raced around the house.

The servant lay rigid on the rock veranda. When he saw that the figure in the dark was Dad, he began to settle down.

"What's wrong? What's wrong?" asked Dad. "Are you sick?"

The man explained as best he could that he had been sleeping when he was grabbed by the throat and his head was pounded into the floor.

Dad checked his throat and, sure enough, there were hand marks on his neck, along with finger nail marks set deeply into the flesh. The poor man wanted no more of this kind of happening and in a moment he had grabbed his lantern and was gone.

"What on earth happened? What did you find?"

Mom was sitting up on her cot shaking from fear when Dad returned. "It's that occult thing. I'm just sure of it," Dad whispered. "I'll betcha one thing. That guy'll never be back, nor will any of his friends."

It so happened that he did come back—the following day; standing on the road and calling through the gate for someone to get him his bed roll. Hearing him, Ted ran to get his possessions and brought them out to him.

A few nights later, our family was having supper. I had Ketchup on my lap and was instructing her on how to eat properly, when I heard a "*ggrrrr.*"

I looked up, and in the cubbyhole of the wall behind Mom and Dad that Ted and I faced when eating, I saw Tootsi, a stray cat that we had recently adopted.

She again made the noise without any provocation. I decided to just watch her, without bringing any attention to her, and see what would happen. She kept on growling and soon there was foam gathering in her mouth. Ted now heard her, and he brought it to our folk's attention.

The low growl continued and escalated slowly into what was eventually a high pitched scream, higher and higher.

We all watched as the foam bubbled, spreading out of the cubbyhole and down the wall. This was getting too much.

Dad finally shooed Tootsi out of the wall and out of the house. We listened to the screaming as it gradually faded down the alley and into the outside world.

We never saw Tootsi again.

~ sixteen ~

Our New Home

Ted and I would check out the sounds each night ...
Just about sundown the laughing hyenas
and jackals would start up.

The great day finally arrived—the day that we were to move into the new house. The Rajah had seen to it that it would be a large house, a veranda around the sides and front. There was a large living room right square in the middle of the house with an adjoining dining room and kitchen. On each side of the living room was a bedroom and bathroom. To the side of one bedroom was a nice and airy office for Dad. Part of the house consisted of a sidewalk stretching about 30 ft behind the kitchen to a building of three rooms.

The first room was for a cooking spot (having the stoves in the house made it just too hot). The second one was for wood to feed the stoves and the third was a garage for the car. And to finish it all off was an upstairs—one that you wouldn't believe. To get to it we had to go to the left veranda, there find a stairwell, climb it to a terrace, right on top of the house, walk across the terrace and into a room enclosed with screening. There, we had three beds —one large one for Dad and Mom, and two smaller ones for Ted and me.

Oh, how Ted and I loved that upstairs. It was high enough to catch the night breezes and the night sounds.

Just behind the house was an area that had at one time claimed to be a mango grove. It was enclosed by a heavy border of hedge growth--cactus, all kinds of thorn trees and jungle growth. It was a favorite home for snakes of every kind. And beyond this was a vast jungle area of night time noises that would waft into our sleeping room.

Ted and I would check out the sounds each night and argue over the origin of new sounds. Just about sundown the laughing hyenas and jackals would start up. Should one of us go to bed in a disgruntled attitude, we would invariably change as we listened to the laughing coming to us from the chorus of hyenas.

We had many pigeons living in the mango trees around our house. They, too, would retreat about sundown, along

Dad in front of our Nuzvid home

with many other kinds of birds. And so it was when all of these various kinds of birds would call it quits for the day they would start looking for a lodging spot for the night. What a squawking bunch they were. Finally they would find a place and settle down. Then we would hear a little twiddling and chirping as they shared with one another the exciting times of the day. And that would be the last we heard from them.

Occasionally, however, during the middle of the night, we would be awakened by a loud squawking – a flutter of wings and then silence. That, we knew, to be the last of a bird thanks to a civet cat or a snake.

***

Itinerating trips! That's when missionaries would go out to camp in the jungle villages and try to convert the villagers to the Gospel. And if you were also supporting a mission school it gave you a chance to tell the people how their children could learn to read and write. How we loved them–Ted and I.

Once every two or three months Dad and Mom would decide that a trip was in order–due to a low count of students at the school. They would get out a map of the territory and come to a decision as to what area needed more representation.

Ted and I had our favorites, and we were happy to express our choice of where to go–Malapardu being our all out favorite.

A number of these villages were supplied with a traveler's bungalow by the British government. Thereby giving aid and comfort to the British representative whose job it was to see that the locals stayed happy and well. If in need, it was determined that Americans could stay in these bungalows also thereby making it possible for our family to reside in them at any time when not in use by the British. This was truly a help to us and other missionaries.

"OK, Kiddos," announced Dad one day. "Tomorrow we are going on a trip....to Conapuram. I am just announcing it early so you'll be ready to go when the time comes."

"Are we taking our camping set up," Ted interrupted, "or is it going to be a bungalow?"

"A bungalow."

This was our first time to this spot, and Ted and I were anxious to see what it was like.

We found that Mosha was going to go with us and that was always a plus for any trip. Mosha was a young boy that came to us from the village–he was an outcast but a very bright kid with a happy disposition – about seventeen years old. Mom trained him carefully to become a good cook.

The next day we arrived in Conapuram anxious to see the home that we would be utilizing for a few days.

It was a pretty house built under some huge trees where a family of monkeys resided. The monkeys seemed happy to see someone filling up the house. They would scoot down the trees and hop over to where we were holding some bread for them. They would come up close, showing their teeth. Then, if any of us would make the slightest movement, scatter back to their trees chattering wildly.

Cautiously, slowly we noticed that the longer they stayed near us the more friendly they became, going so far as to take the food right out of our hands.

Along about the second day Ted and I decided to play catch with a big ball that we had brought from home. I had also brought Ketchup out to watch the game, placing her in the crook of a tree and hoping that the monkey family wouldn't see her, but not so. The daddy of the family decided to check her out. Silently he padded over to take a closer look. A moment later when I glanced up, he was holding her by her beautiful blond hair inspecting every inch of her. I let out a yell,

"Noooo!"

The frightened monkey threw the doll and ran for a tree. By the time I reached Ketchup she was a sorry looking sight. With Mom's help, I took her into the house and cleaned her up as best we could.

Ted soon called that we hadn't finished our game of catch. So I left Ketchup in Mom's care and returned to our game.

Somewhere in our rowdy bump and jostle with the ball Ted & I both took a tumble. Sliding in a hole, we noticed a strange feeling. It was like a dark shadow was passing over us. A moment later our heads felt as though they were on fire. Itching. Scratching. And burning!

Screaming loudly we dashed into the house and yelling for Dad - who immediately noticed the cloud of fleas taking up residence on our bodies.

Dashing for a rag and lantern, he began rubbing kerosene onto our heads, while mom did her best to comfort our stinging panic.

Following inspection it turned out that we had been invaded by enough fleas to populate a thousand circuses, but we never found out why they had taken over the hole ... and our family.

Before it was all over, all four of us found ourselves soaking in kerosene... everyone that is but Ketchup.

Front row: Punkie, Ted, Freddie and me.
Second row: Dr. Emma Hughes, Maude Coyne, unknown, and Mom.
Third row: Pastor Cormack, President of Seventy-day Adventists in India, Dr. Coyne, unknown, and Dad.

~ seventeen ~

Collette

"Collette, please, please come back and sit under the table with us. Tell us the funny jokes again. Don't go. Please don't go."

About noon one day, a bicycle appeared on the edge of the compound. A young man parked it, came to the house, and knocked on the front door. When Mother opened the door he handed her a letter. Mom read the page, then whispered a name, *"...Collette."*

***

When we left for America and returned to India Dad was still responsible for the mission work being done in the Narsapur field. The school there was growing, and the medical field was in its own way expanding. So The General Conference added to the Narsapur staff a young doctor and his wife, Adrian Clark and....Collette.

Ted and I decided that they were the perfect couple for the job.

One day Dad had decided he had to visit Narsapur, and he asked the rest of the family to join him on the journey. We were ecstatic to visit our old home.

Upon meeting the Clarks we were amazed that they were not only so 'at home' in the jungle but also so 'comfortable' around kids.

No denying it. They loved us.

For our visit Collette planned a wonderful dinner, and the cooking lady was serving it splendidly. When dessert time came Ted gave me that 'look' which meant, "Follow me." With a sense of adventure I nodded and watched him closely.

There was a large tablecloth covering the table, the corners almost reaching the floor. Quietly, he pulled up the corner of the cloth and slipped underneath. I looked at the grown-ups to see what their reaction would be, but they were so busy talking that they seemed totally unaware. So, I picked up my corner of the tablecloth, and when the conversation got a little heavy I slipped below and waited for the reaction.

After a moment...

"I swear, Honey, the kids were just here! Where could they have gone? How embarrassing."

Then after another brief silence, we heard Collette's voice.

"You know what folks it is so hot, I think that I'll just get down on the floor where it's at least 2 or 3 degrees cooler."

Just then we saw the tablecloth lift and down came Collette.

"Well, hi kids. Looks like you had the same idea I did," she whispered, with a big grin and a wink. Settling herself on the floor, she leaned up against a table leg. From there she directed her cook to serve us under the table.

What a ball the three of us had - sharing a fabulous vanilla pudding with a smattering of jokes by an impressive jokester. From then on nothing could deflect our loyalty to Collette. Absolutely nothing!

But then came the letter....

She was no more. How could that be? Collette, please, please come back and sit under the table with us. Tell us the funny jokes again. Don't go. Please don't go.

Hearing the news I vanished to another room, and I saw Ted take off to parts unknown. I was young and didn't understand the meaning of death. *Why? Oh why did this have to happen? Happen to someone that I loved so much?*

1st row: Ted, Freddie, Punkie & me
2nd row: Dr. Adrian Clark, Mom, Mable Schutt,
Collette Clark,
Maude Coyne, Dr. Hughes
3rd row: Cecil Clark (*he and Mable ran the school in Narsapur*),
Dad, unknown, & Dr. Coyne

After what seemed like hours my Mom came to find me. She put her arms around me and hugged me tight, and in her kind way she explained to me the meaning of death.

"One day you will get to see Auntie Collette again, and you can spend as much time with her as you want." Mom brushed some loose hairs out of my eyes. "Tomorrow we will be going to her funeral, in Narsapur, and I want you to remember all during the funeral that you *will* see her again....Will you remember that?"

Collette lay in a wooden box out on the veranda of our old house. There were the very few white people who were serving in that area along side of the native folk who made up the school and the clinic. And sitting over by the coffin was Dr. Adrian. How sorry I felt for him. His head was down and his eyes closed. Every few minutes he would take from his pocket a hanky and blow his nose with it.

I was sure that he was thinking about when it happened. It happened so quickly—just the day before...

Collette was getting ready to go to the clinic for the day, when she had this awful pain in her tummy. Mentioning it to Adrian, he told her to be sure and follow it carefully.

Along about noon the pain got so bad that she could stand it no longer. He decided that he needed to 'go in' and see what was wrong. What he found was a baby growing in the fallopian tube.

He tried to rectify the situation, but in the process Collette died on the table.

Pastor Losby was trying now to give a coherent funeral service, but he kept breaking down, along with most of the people there.

Finally we all sang a hymn, and they closed the box. Eight men carried the casket out to a spot in the front yard, where a hole had been dug. We all followed the group.

Dad offered a final prayer. The box was let down and handfuls of dirt were dropped on it—that being the final act.

As we walked away from the burial spot, a canal boat was gliding by with the pullers singing a sweet melody. The blending of the voices—theirs with ours— seemed to cast a blessing on the occasion—a blessing that all of us could share.

~ eighteen ~

Tommy Tucker

"I just can't figure out why Tom would take off with those no good friends of his."

"Did you hear that squeaking sound?" Ted pointed toward the stairs. "Oh. Oh. There it goes again." Pin-pointing the *'squeak'* we realized it was coming from atop a pillar out on the veranda. Using a nearby chair, Ted placed it at the base of the column and climbed to the top. There in a recessed niche about a foot and a half wide he spied a nest! It was made of feathers, little bits of cloth, and soft kinds of weeds. Carefully Ted peeked into the cubby nest and spied baby chipmunks.

"What do we do with them?" Together we ran into Dad's office.

"Come and see what we just found!" Dutifully Dad followed us out onto the veranda and stepped up on the chair.

"What do you know," Dad grinned, "Three tiny chipmunks."

"Can we take them down and give them something to eat? Please!"

"Tell you what," Dad replied in a reasoned tone. "We don't know what's happened to their mother. If we touch her babies she won't have anything to do with them again. Why don't we just let them stay here until tomorrow morning? If she hasn't come to take care of them by then we will know that she won't be coming back."

Ted and I groused our way to bed that night, and in the morning we were the first ones to awake.

It was barely light when I heard Ted sneaking out of bed and tiptoeing to the stairs. I then watched him climb the chair and look into the nest.

Squeak. Squeak. Squeak.

"The mother isn't here," he announced. "Bet that means she met up with a civet cat yesterday."

Upon hearing the news Dad suggested that we carefully take down the nest and bring the little chipmunks into the kitchen, where we would decide together what we should do for the little things.

They had no hair. Their eyes had not opened yet. The trio was each about two and a half inches long. It was hard to believe that such insignificant looking little things could make a sound capable of catching anyone's attention. But here we were, trying to decide if there was any chance to save them.

"O.K. Junie," Dad nodded, "you be the name maker."

"Let's see, the first one is...Corkie. The big one is Tommy Tucker, and the little guy is...Benjie."

Immediately Ted and I set about to make a home for the three little orphans. We found a box—about the size of an average apple crate and lined it with an old sheet. Inside of that we put the nest their missing mother constructed, fluffy and soft.

Dad got some buffalo milk and a medicine dropper. He sucked up some milk in the dropper—about one fourth and then filled up the rest of the dropper with warm water. Ever so carefully he picked up one of the chipmunks and put the dropper to his face. The poor little thing was so hungry and thirsty that he just sucked and sucked as best he could, with much of the milk running down the outside of his tummy.

Each one was given the same breakfast and then laid down for a nap.

In an hour or so Ted decided that it was surely dinner time again so he started getting out the essentials. Dad heard the commotion and came to investigate.

"We need to give them some time to rest, Buddy. Let's give 'em three hours between feeding times. Every three hours, does that sound about right to you, Ted?" My brother relaxed his impatient shoulders and reluctantly nodded.

The first day went well. And the second. As the third morning dawned Ted and I, as usual, tried to beat each other to the chipmunk box. When we got there only Tommy Tucker and Corkie were squeaking. Little Benjie was quiet and still. Ted pushed him with his finger, but he didn't respond.

"What's wrong with him?" I whispered.

"Don't know. He might be dead?" Ted's tone changed. "Think I'll pick him up and see." Sure enough, he was gone.

Hiding his sadness he set his mind to planning a Christian funeral; Dad would present the sermon and Mom would provide the special music. All of this was decided without consulting our parents. So, by the time they heard of the project, it was already funeral time.

They did ask for ten minutes extra – to prepare for the momentous occasion.

The servants were given a few moments to drop the projects that they were doing and told to meet out behind the garage. When they arrived they found an arrangement of short logs on which to sit. Before them lay Benjie in a tiny box lined with some nice white office paper.

When the group was seated, Ted announced that Mother was going to provide the special music. I was afraid, at first, that Mom couldn't handle it—for a long moment she stared at the ground, trying to suppress her smile. Then with an understanding voice she led us in a verse of "Jesus Loves Me This I Know."

Glancing at Pillau—the buffalo keeper—I saw that he had his hand over his mouth to hide his amusement.

Ted thanked Mom and announced that Dad would pronounce the sermon. Dad did a great job—short and to the point.

Remembering at the last second that a prayer always finishes a meeting, Ted
turned to me.

"A-and eh...n-n-now we'll ask June to have the closing prayer."

"Nooo... I can't." I glared at him, trying not to be obvious.

"Sure you can," he whispered back, just as petrified as me. Then turning once more to face his backyard congregation, he added,

"Let's just bow our heads and close our eyes."

Silence. More silence. Then just as it became unbearable, a kindly voice called out to God, "We ask your blessings on us all."

"Thank you, Dad," I signed under my breath, *"Thank you."*

Five days later there was only one voice left: Tommy Tucker's. Little Corkie had met with Benjie's fate and was given the same respectful send off.

When it became apparent that Tommy Tucker was going to live—(he was getting bigger and stronger by the day), Dad and Ted decided it was time to make him a permanent home. They took the box that he was in and fastened it to the kitchen window. They made a door that could be opened and closed, and tied it to the window bars (all of the windows were covered with heavy bars protecting the house from thieves). They upholstered the cardboard residence making one fourth of the box a luxurious king-sized (in chipmunk talk) bed.

When it was agreed that Tommy was big enough, the chipmunk was moved into his new accommodations.

"But what if Tommy wakes up scared and doesn't know where he is? What if he just takes off and we lose him?" Ted voiced his concerns.

"I think that we should try him out for one night," Dad suggested. "Ted will stay with him. Being near Tommy through the night will give him a lot of comfort."

"Can I stay with him too?" I asked.

"Two would make it better than one."

For the first few nights Ted and I slept right below the chipmunk box. I didn't think that we should leave the door open, but Ted and Dad felt that he would be safe – that he wouldn't run away. After some fussing I relented and the door stayed open. I chose to be the first guard and stay awake for the first three hours while Ted slept then he would guard while I slept, and so it would go.

As it turned out we were both sound asleep by morning, and Tommy was chewing on a cashew nut totally indifferent to the surrounding area. From then on we didn't worry about Tommy leaving. Instead we took him from the box, rubbed his back, and gave him something tasty to eat and dropped him on the window sill. We watched with bated breath to see which way he would go. We saw him step-one foot out-and one foot back. He put his nose in the air and sniffed this way and that. Then he looked up to see the towel hanging from his box to the sill below where he was standing. He stepped onto the towel and started his climb up looking much pleased with himself on the way. He found the opening to the box and came on in.

For many days he would not leave his box but instead waited to be picked up and carried out. And now we would carry him a little bit farther away each day, placing him down and letting him find his way back. During this time he was getting bigger and bigger – his tail becoming truly beautiful. He would sit and chirp flicking his tail up and down, up and down. As the days passed by we noticed a beginning familiarity with the local chipmunks. On their part it was a curiosity that had given itself away by looking intently at this beautiful big new chipmunk in their midst.

One morning we were surprised to see where Tommy had, on his own, exited the chipmunk cage and was off now playing somewhere with the local chipmunks. Or at least we hoped he was. Since he had joined us we had taken a much closer look at what chipmunks do every day. Where do they go during the day? What do they eat? Who are their friends? Their enemies?

As we were standing there looking for Tommy we heard a smattering of chipmunk talk. It was coming this way from the roof top. We looked up and saw about five or maybe six chipmunks heading for the cage. Ted suggested that we back up and pay no attention to the crowd. This we did and on they came. The biggest one—the one with the prettiest tail and talking the most just had to be Tommy. He led the way and into the cage.

"Whoa," said the next chipmunk (in chipmunk talk of course), "that's not for me." Sure enough they all stood at the cage opening waiting for Tommy to move. Tom groused around in the cage for a few minutes, and then realizing that the others were not going to follow him into his home, he took off - up and over the roof top with the new found friends following closely behind. Each one chattered just as loudly as he could. "What do you think, Sis, are they coming back?"

I was afraid that we had seen the last of Tommy. He was drawn to his new friends more than he was to us. His little box now seemed quiet and empty. All of the chattering was gone. If he should hear the cry of a hawk how would he know it was a noise to stay away from? Would his friends be aware that he should be told of such things?

All day long I fretted about Tommy. Would he remember where home was? Would he remember where there was food for him? Along about noon I decided to go out into the mango grove and look for him. I remembered having seen chipmunks in groups playing in the trees – far from the house. I would go and see.

Up and down, up and down the lines of trees I would go – looking for Tommy. In about an hour I came across Ted who was doing the same thing.

"I just can't figure out why Tom would take off with those no good friends of his." Ted kicked an ant hill with his toe giving emphasis to his statement. "We give him everything he needs–or even wants, and he just runs off. That's appreciation for ya."

Supper time came, and we were sick with worry. Mom and Dad tried hard to interest us in the menu but it was just a 'no go.' Was it a hawk, a civet cat, or did he just lose the way? But then what difference does it really make? If he's gone, he's gone. It was then that the tears started coming.

"He's here! He's here!" shouted Mosha bursting in the door. "Come see! Come see!" We dashed out the back door and there was this big, beautiful chipmunk looking for food in his home box. I was so excited that I just grabbed Tommy and hugged and hugged him. In time I gave him over to Ted, and he had his turn of hugging. Up on the roof was the rest of the chipmunk party chirping away and evidently saying goodnight to Tommy.

The next day I was walking to the outside kitchen when all of a sudden a big chipmunk came up behind me, jumped onto my shorts, climbed onto my shirt, and up to my shoulder. It lay there across my shoulder for maybe fifteen minutes then chirped, gave a big jump, landed safely on the ground—and disappeared around the corner of the house. I followed him quietly wanting to see where he was headed.

For a moment he stopped at the doorway to Dad's office. Peeking in I saw that Dad had two men folk that he was conversing with. They were startled by Tommy's intrusion and sat staring with mouths wide open. Tom was chirping, flicking his tail up and down evidently trying to determine the height of the desk. No problem. With one mighty jump he cleared the desk coming down halfway across the top. Going into reverse gear he came to a stop just short of the far edge.

The men were agog. They jumped from their chairs and headed for the door when one of them decided that it would be much more interesting to see what would happen next. Tommy started sniffing around examining the different things he found on top of the desk. When he got to Dad he noticed that there was a hole—an opening between the buttons—the fourth and fifth button on his shirt.

Dad noted the trouble that he was having trying to get into the shirt so he quietly opened button number four, thus making the hole much wider. (Noting how much easier it was for Tommy to enter his shirt with the button gone, he decided to open it every time he saw Tommy at his office door.)

Cautiously he sniffed the area putting one foot into the space, sniffed some more, and in went the next foot. Hey, this was great. The opening just kept going. On around Dad's waist he ventured but when he got to Dad's center back he decided that this would make a cool bed – something that he just couldn't pass by. It took a few minutes for Tommy to settle in for a nap – pushing the shirt material this way and that, lying down after every shift to see if this time it was just right.

Dad always got larger shirts than average. It was his way of helping to beat the heat. Tommy's appreciation was evident, for by the time he was ready to lie down and go to sleep he had pushed out a large area of space in the shirt material hanging over the belt. Dad's grimacing settled down as Tommy settled in for a nap.

This procedure began to be a habit. Practically every day Tommy would forsake his friends out in the trees and would scamper in to Dad's office, stop momentarily at the door, chatter up a storm, and scare anyone who was there. Then quietly he would jump to the desk top, and sedately tip toe over to Dad's shirt and disappear for approximately 30 to 40 minutes. Ted and I so loved to see the reaction of the people who would see Tommy for the first time that we would beg Dad to let us do our school work in his office. He was kind and gave in quite often. There we would sit on the floor across the room from Dad. Usually we would do the school work in one of our tree houses located in a big mango tree, but this was just too much fun to pass by.

One day I was out feeding my chicken—a mommy with about a dozen little baby chicks—when Tommy came up to me chattering and flipping his tail. He obviously wanted something so I reached down to pick him up, and he went limp in my hand. I looked down. His eyes were shut, and he looked sound asleep. Well, this was a new way of sleeping I decided. It was going to be a challenge—but I noted that there was a big pocket in my apron that I filled up with chicken feed and continued to throw it around for mommy hen and her little ones. She was grousing big time and following me closely. Suddenly she gave a big squawk and lunged for Tommy's tail. Too late I pulled him up as his beautiful tail disappeared from sight. I was horrified. As fast as I could I ran to Dad's office with Tommy in both hands. From a bony appendage he was dripping blood all over the desk.

"What can we do, Dad? Is he going to die? He can't die. He just can't."

"Keep holding him for a minute," said Dad, as he ran to the bedroom to fetch the ever ready bottle of mercurochrome. When he returned he took Tommy, dunked his tail into the bottle, and swished it around. Gently he took Tom to his box and laid him down onto the clean nest material. Tom was whimpering softly.

We were so relieved that he didn't want to find his friends and scamper around the mango grove but instead was satisfied to lie quietly. This continued for about three or four days. We could see the skin gradually take hold on the bone and then tiny hairs started to reappear. As his tail was recouping, we noticed that he was getting more and more interested in the outside world. And then one morning he headed out to catch his friends and to find the world that had left him behind. I should say right here that in time Tommy's tail had again become his pride and joy as it grew much larger than any of his friends in the mango grove.

~ nineteen ~

Bearded Toads & BB's Before Bed

"*Good grief!*" Mother gasped, walking into the room.
"*What is this, Ted?
A bunch of handicapped...toads!?*"

It was a hot day in April when Mom brought up the subject. "June, you and Ted seem to have quite a time getting to sleep every night. You're getting older so how about adding a half hour to your get-to-bed time? That would help you to beat the heat a bit." In my delight I ran to find Ted and share with him the great news.

That night when the chore work was all done and the dining room table was cleared Mom went to her desk that sat in the downstairs bedroom. Out of a drawer she pulled a bunch of papers. From his desk in his office, Dad did likewise. Together they spread out the material onto the dining room table and went to work. Correspondence for Mom. Office work for Dad. This was a scene that we, Ted and I, seldom saw, for we were close to bed when dinner was over. How do we spend that half extra hour gift? Just about then we saw a big toad hopping through the dining room door. He was lunging at flies, mosquitoes, and ants as he came.

"Watch out, Sis, I've got a really great idea. Just follow me."

What did Ted have in mind I wondered? Something to do with the toad? He disappeared for a few minutes returning with a little box of something or another. He slid under the dining room table which was really quite large. I followed and watched as he began to open the box. From it he took out a handful of BB shots – little round metal balls – the ones that fired up our BB gun. As I searched for a comfortable place to sit down I saw that Ted was motioning to me. He had his index finger to his lips—indicating to me to be quiet. Then he pointed to the toad that had just about made it to the table.

The toad was busy grabbing airborne insects along with those that crawled on the stone floors.

From his one hand Ted took a nice round shiny BB, carefully aiming it toward the toad and letting go. Slowly – very slowly – it edged toward the frog. It was fun watching the frog see it for the first time. He slowly positioned himself to catch it first off. Then his long tongue flashed out and wrapped itself around the ball. Oops. Out it fell. Again he tried. This time it worked, and he was ready to catch another. And another. And still another.

Wow! What a supper he was having. And here came another toad. A big one—probably six to seven inches long. Ted was having a blast supplying them both with all of his metal nourishment. By now number one was getting a little sluggish. When he would see a BB coming toward him he would jump toward it but somehow his tummy just wouldn't follow through with the plan. With his front feet he would try to crawl toward the ball and drag his tummy with him. This worked for a little while, but then all movement stopped.

"What do we do now?" asked Ted. Number two was beginning to slow down also. It was obvious that we were beginning to face a problem.

"Hey, I know," Ted's eyes brightened. "Why didn't I think of it before? Just watch!"

With that announcement Ted reached out and took hold of the toad's back feet and held him upside down. Out of his mouth slid all of the BB's that we had fed him. Not only that but he was struggling to get back to them again. We picked up the BB's and started serving supper all over again. That first night two more toads joined the party before Mom called it bedtime.

"You guys have been having fun with those toads, haven't you? I'll give you ten more minutes to finish up then worship and off to bed. Sound O.K.? "

"Great."

She did not have a hint of recognition as to what we were doing with the toads. Ted and I were elated. "Hey, Sis, we can carry on again tomorrow night just like tonight. Great or what?" he whispered.

The following night the toads started coming earlier. All together there were five. During the day Ted had been thinking of new ways to feed them.

How about soap!? "It might have some nourishment -- well, something good in it. Think I'll try it out." Ted looked satisfied with himself.

"Hey, Sis, where does Mom get the pretty pink soap we're using in the bathroom just now? You know. The kind that smells so good?"

"It's a really special kind. It comes from America," I answered.

"Tell you what. I'll get you a knife and you can cut little balls from it. It's such pretty stuff, I'm sure that it must taste good too." By supper time I had a bowl full of little balls cut from a bar of soap. Proud of it, I offered it to Ted who hid it under a living room pillow.

Following supper the first two frogs came in the door together, and Ted was busy catching insects for them. In short order he got out the dish of soap and chose a nice clean ball. He pitched it toward one of the toads who lunged for it, and zap it was gone. Another followed, and another.

Now it was time to start on number two toad. Oh, how he did love that soap. He was bouncing all over the under part of the table. Oops. Here comes two more toads. Ted was running out of soap balls, but he did have a good number of BB balls left in his pocket which he started using. Before long the room started looking like a bar scene of drunken toads, each one supporting a long beard of soapy bubbles. Add to that a toad tummy that could scarcely move, and you had a pretty pathetic and hilarious sight.

"Good grief!" Mother gasped, walking into the room. "What's going on under the table?" Pushing the chair back to get a better look, she pointed. "What is this, Ted, a bunch of handicapped...toads?"

"Really, Mom, it's not as bad as it looks. See here, I can fix the ones that can't walk." With that he picked up one of the toads by his back legs and out gushed the BB's. Now the frog was happy and proceeded to chase after the little balls trying to get them back into his tummy, again.

"And the beards?" Dad chimed in from the doorway, "Some fuzzy soap?" As he tried to form the word "soap," Dad could hold back the laughter no longer. Mom caught it from him, and in a moment all four of us were laughing up a storm. When we finally settled down Dad tried to talk, but it took him awhile. Looking at the drunken toads would start him all over again.

"Now listen, Kids," said Dad as he tried to maintain his composure..."I....I just....uh..." He turned his head so we wouldn't see he was still in stitches. "Let's see that it just doesn't... uh... doesn't happen again, O.K.?"

~ *twenty* ~

Mosha Gets the Boot

"Oh my goodness!" The pastor cried out,
"My leg! What's happened to my leg?"

Ted and I held to a rather loosely controlled school plan. We had no school books as such, so Dad or Mom would sketch up a paper of math questions, and we would count that day as math class. Or we would be given a storybook for reading which then would be considered our Literature lesson. We had no schoolhouse, but we could choose between two locations for the day—either our tree house in the mango grove or Dad's office. We had no chairs in the office, but instead told Dad that we would much rather sit on the floor with our backs to the wall—like our friends did in the village.

An advantage of the tree house was that Tommy Tucker would usually find us and join our class—spread out on the floor sound asleep. And of course, Ketchup was always with me during school time.

The advantage of choosing the office was that we could hear all of the "goings on" of the place when folks came in to talk to Dad. But if there was something that Dad felt that we shouldn't hear we would be detoured to the mango grove.

One day Ted and I were in the office working on some math when the man from the telegraph office came by with a message for Dad. The note indicated that on the following Monday an Elder West would be arriving in Nuzvid on the afternoon train. He would be coming to see how the work was coming along in our area of India. It also noted that Elder West was from Australia.

It was exciting, of course, to have a white person come to Nuzvid—to visit us but still.......a little bit on the scary side. What do they wear? What do they eat? What interests them to talk about? Well, we had five more days before he would be coming so not to worry.

There was a mango tree standing just in front of the house. On it was a lovely big branch stretching out over the driveway, quite hidden from people walking beneath. This was our welcoming pad. We would wait until we heard the motor car coming around the bend of the road from the hospital. We would then scurry out on the branch to check out the company as the car stopped right below us.

It was now Monday afternoon and all was in readiness for the arrival of Elder West. The folks had gone to the train station to fetch him home, and we were sitting on the branch waiting to check him out.

"Fine place you got here, Folks." Elder West was surveying the compound as he extracted a suitcase from the car. Mosha and Dad were helping him in his efforts, and shortly thereafter they were all seated in the living room exchanging niceties.

What we could hear of the conversation sounded fascinating —kangaroos. Yep, this man was actually from the land of kangaroos, and we didn't want to miss a beat. So as shy as we were we decided to brave the situation. In a hurry we climbed down from the tree, and Dad introduced us along with Mosha.

"Mosha, I wonder if you would do something for me," Elder West asked through Dad's translation.

"Yes, Sir?"

"Take a hold of my boot and pull it off please. My feet are soooo hot." And with that he held up one of his boots for Mosha to grab.

Being a bit on the timid side, Mosha took hold of the boot rather gingerly and gave it a little pull.

"You'll have to really pull, Mosha."

Again Mosha tugged. Nothing.

"You look like a strong boy," Elder West encouraged. "This time take hold and really give it a yank."

Mustering all of his strength Mosha grabbed hold of the boot and waited for its owner to give him the signal.

"One...Two...Three...Pull!"

No mistake this time. Mosha gave it all he had. And not only did he pull off the boot -- he took Elder's leg with him as well. Mosha tumbled over backward–once, twice and came to rest next to a booted leg.

"Oh my goodness!" the pastor cried out, "My leg! What's happened to my leg?"

Mosha was overwhelmed —beside– himself, next to the leg. Coming to himself, he grabbed the appendage and headed for the door.

"Wait a minute! Boy! Come back here. Bring my leg!"

Watching the scene I was just as flustered as Mosha, thinking our guest was suddenly maimed. This was all just too terrible to think about.

As I turned to follow Mosha out the door, I heard a heavy boom of laughter. It couldn't be the Pastor? How? Why?

Daring to steal a glance over my shoulder, my unbelieving eyes were met by the sight of a one-legged man overcome by...laughter.

Slowly, ever so slowly, Ted, Mosha, and I made our way over to the Pastor. He reached out and took his leg from Mosha.

"See here, Boy. This is how it's fixed." With that introduction, he explained the workings of an artificial leg to three wide-eyed kids.

~ *twenty-one* ~

The Magic Spell of Dungula

Sitting near Dad I heard him say to the car,
"Hey, no letting us down out here. Nooooooo flat tires or motor problems, do you hear?"

One day at supper time Dad shared some news with Ted and me. Mom was away in Madras at the English hospital getting some tests done. The question was did she have some tropical disease, and if she did what to do to overcome it.

Dad continued, "I just have so much typing to do. I have reams and reams of catching up on journals, and I was thinking that if we could just go to Malapardu for a few days I could probably catch up there. What do you think?"

"Whoopee! Whoopee!" shouted Ted. "I'm sure that you could get it all done at Malapardu." I joined in the chorus and in a few minutes the problem was settled. We were on our way to Molapardu.

This was Ted and my very, very favorite itinerant spot. (An itinerate spot is simply a camp-out place where missionaries go to do a mission project). First of all there was Sobinathery—an old hunter who was the hero of the village. He was never in such a hurry that he couldn't take the time to tell us a story, one that could fit the situation to a "T."

One of our favorite stories was about Dad and two tigers in the Malapardu area. Dad was quite new to that area and when asked by the villagers of Malapardu if he would please, please come and save their cattle, he just couldn't turn them away. The story happened before Ted and I were old enough to be along on the hunt. So we could only imagine ourselves to be there when he pulled the trigger. One tiger, when hit, roared itself into a thicket of cactus bushes much too thick for anyone to follow. There it stayed for several hours until its roaring could be heard no more. The other tiger was evidently not hit for it disappeared into the jungle and was not seen again.

The village of Malapardu is located at the foot of a long range of hills. And from this point there is a rather major roadway leading out of the area heading west. The road connects a number of villages in the area and is greatly depended on by the residents of these places, Malipardu included. But in the event that you might think of it as a grand highway polished by present day asphalt you are mistaken. For these "main roads" are merely cleared jungle to a width wide enough for buffaloes, camels, sheep, and goats to pass each other. From Malapardu there is a path heading for the hill country, and this trail is kept up by hand. But I suppose, if asked, "What is the most intriguing aspect, to you, about Maulapardu," we would have to admit that along with the tigers and leopards is the mysterious village, far into the interior of these mountains, called Dunglavaribaye. This village had the distinct mystery of being made up entirely of thieves.

"Why? Why are they allowed?" Dad asked the head man of the area.

"Their religion makes way for a caste of thieves, and these people on the whole feel that living as they do in a hideaway spot in the mountains makes them a bother to no one."

"Someday, Dad, we're gonna have to go up and check in on them." Ted sounded determined. Every month or two they will have a village get-together to determine just where they should go on their next village raid. They have sent spies ahead who have checked out where the thieves will stay during the nights and retreat times on the job. If a policeman catches one of the thieves while he is raiding – he is in big trouble. All of the thieves are anonymous to the villagers for they never come around on a normal basis. So you can see how they can remain unnoticed, unsuspected, and unknown."

I well remember how exciting it was when the thieves would come to Nuzvid. This would happen once every two or three years. The stories were always wild and frightening. About five miles to the north of Nuzvid there is a mountain called Suthikundra (or Needle Mountain). When night would fall and it had been a particularly busy day in the office or maybe just a hot day, Dad or Mom would get inspired to hop into the car and go for a spin in the jungle. Cool off a bit.

On the front upper part of the car was mounted a strong spotlight, which Dad could use very handily. With it he could easily pick up a wild boar, hyena, leopard, or tiger. Usually on these treks he would take a gun for protection. Because the British ruled India at the time, the Indian natives were not allowed to own a gun, so when a tiger or leopard killed the villager's livestock they would come to Dad to ask him to kill the offending animal. But Dad was always very careful to not exhaust the big cats of the jungle.

Only on a crisis case, when the village was losing its herds, would he comply. And Malapardu seemed to always be a crisis case – over-run by leopards and tigers.

One night Dad called out, "Who wants to go to Suthikundra?"

Ted was quick on the draw. "You bet, Dad. But why are we going?"

"There was a fellow down from Lakawadum in the office today, and he was saying that he had caught sight of a tiger out by the mountain. I thought it just might be fun to see if we could catch a glimpse of him, too."

Ted and I caught our favorite car seats (the two front fenders), and we were on our way. When we reached Suthikundra Dad had us get in the car, and we took a little trail off from the main road. Dad turned on the search light. This was the exciting time–Dad searching for eyes that we could see as clearly as he. Usually the animal would be mildly interested in the light – stare at it momentarily then continue with whatever he had been doing. We saw a variety of different kinds of animals, but not the tiger.

Dad made the comment that there wasn't much activity going on tonight when he turned the car around a little curve in the trail and there in front of us were the thieves of Dungula. They had no fire. No light. We could see probably about twelve of them. They were getting ready for the night. Their surprise was equal to ours.

Dad suddenly realized what a sad situation we were in. He had forgotten that there was a raid on the village or he would never have made this trip. As fast as he could he was turning the car around and then he would head for the main road. Getting the car turned around was a major hurdle in this jungle. The race now was between the thieves getting some branches strewn across the trail to stop us – or our getting the car turned around first.

"What'll they do to us, Daddy? What'll they do?"

"Don't worry, Honey. We'll make it. We'll make it." Dad was knocking over little trees that hugged the trail. One large thorn tree was a real obstacle. He kept butting it over and over, but it just wouldn't go down and let us pass. Sitting near Dad I heard him say to the car, "Hey, no letting us down out here. Nooooooo flat tires or motor problems, do you hear?" Backing up he tried again–hitting the–accelerator–and easing ......over ...... over ......o...v....e....r. ... the tree. We were all praying for clear sailing and sure enough God granted us our wish.

The next day the little village newspaper (written in Telegue) was all abuzz with the news of the thieves. Whose homes had they raided? Whom had they clobbered in a fight? Where were they spending the night? One thing they added to the raid was the screamer–the man who ran over the village screaming at the top of his lungs for hours. This he would do many full moon nights. Whenever the night-time police would get near him he would go quiet until he would arrive at the other side of the village and again he would shout at a very high decibel level and the chase would begin again. Ted and I would listen to all the noise with bated breath–hoping that the man would be caught, but then when we realized that he just may be, we hoped that he would get away. On this particular night I awakened Ted with the news that the screamer was near our house.

"Oh my goodness. He sure is," said Ted on awakening. "And it sounds like he is heading to our place. Quick, Sis. Let's get out on the terrace and see if we can see him while he's running by."

Out we scrambled as fast as we could. The screaming got higher and higher. He turned into our back hedge row and here he came. We were watching carefully. We heard him running right below us, but the night was too dark to let us see him and on he ran. As it turned out this was the next to the last night that the thieves were in town. They had various ways of getting home—following little jungle trails singly or in small groups. They had donkeys on which they would carry their loot. Sometimes when the thieves would come to our village, I would wonder why the police had such a hard time catching them. Then, deep down—deep, deep down I would add it up to the fun and the magic that the thieves by their coming would spread over the village of Nuzvid. And then, of course, they had the religious aspect to think about too.

~ twenty-two ~

The Leopard of Malapardu

You have a good strong stick. Put a lot of positive belief in it - when you see a big cat, instead of running off in fear, come at him swinging with that stick, and hope that he will get the idea.

From Malapardu there is a trail heading for the hill country, and this trail is kept up by hand. The first mile of it is covered with scars left from the waters of the monsoon rains. They can become quite deep and distort the balance of the area. So for the car it could bump and grind up to that spot, but no farther. And at that spot was a hill–made of huge boulders–probably about 50 feet high. Hugging close to the trail was a thick jungle hedge that was a good 30 feet wide made up of thorn bushes, thorn trees, and various kinds of jungle out growth. This mile of hedge could not be penetrated anywhere along the line, but here it stopped with the presence of a huge banyan tree creating a perfect place for a camping site. And this was known as OUR place, OUR campsite OUR Malapardu home (Ted and my rendition of the situation anyway). How we loved that spot!

It was always a big day when our car would drive into the village. No one knew of our coming ahead so it was always a surprise. About half of the village would follow our car out toward the campsite and slowly drop back as they tired. But there was a good group that made it to the end each time and was there to help us with the setting up of camp.

Mosha was ecstatic when he heard Dad say that we needed him on the trip. My folks had a whole set-up for Mosha to pack when we took him with us on a trip. The list included a one man tent; cooking utensils; five or six basic cooking supplies such as salt, sugar, buffalo ghee, and flour; sleeping gear, etc. Mosha loved to select his spot for the stay–when a big cat was involved–we noticed that he would be but thirty feet away. But if the trip was solely for meetings—fifty feet would do. In Malapardu Mosha had his very own pad—just inside the hedge opening. About thirty feet on was the family tent spot—right under the banyan tree.

Dad was quick to notice the different kinds of traffic going by—on the trail into the village. Today there were a number of hyena tracks, jackals, wild boar, and one lone bear. Nothing very exciting.

Our tent was approximately 20/20 feet with a flap out in front which gave us added shade. Dad always put his cot out in front of the tent just under the flap with his gun and flash light lying beside of him in case of an emergency. Mother—when she was with us, slept just inside the tent and of course Ted and me taking up the back of the area.

I well remember that first night. We had said our goodnights and gone to sleep. Along about two or three I heard this terrible high pitched "Yeeeooow—yeeeooow." I jumped up to try and figure out what was going on. Dad had the flashlight on – centering the flow toward the back of the tent. He was yelling at the animal trying to scare it at the same time not wanting to scare Ted or me. Just then I saw it flashing by – under my cot – going round and round inside the tent. I recognized it to be a big civet cat. (A civet cat is a wild animal, mean and scrappy, about two or three times bigger than an average American house cat.) Dad had to finally get out of bed to steer it out of the tent. It took awhile before Ted and I could get back to sleep.

The next day Sobanathory came by with his dog. Ted and I had been waiting for this moment for some time now. We took him to the boulder hill - the one that sat right in front of our camp site - found a cozy little place under a tree and asked him to please tell us some stories. This is what he loved to do and when he had shared with us a number of thrilling tales he explained that he needed to check out the night callers first.

The Malipardu people raise a few acres of peanuts and sugar cane which they guard very carefully. It is with the profit from these two crops that the people of the village are able to sustain themselves.

They build a small porch up at about fourteen feet. A ladder goes up on one side with a smattering of blankets to keep them warm through a cold night. Anything that makes noise is also added to the melee. At sundown a man of the village will climb to the top of a stand and spend the night listening for an animal scrounging around in the crop. And when an interloper is heard the first one to hear sets off the chorus – and all join in. This continues for a few minutes, and soon all will feel connected and safe, the animal is frightened off, and the night callers will fall off to sleep again. Sobonathry knew just where each one was located, and we checked them all. Most were in the process of wrapping up the night's activities and finding out how the others had survived.

There was, Sobonathry said, a young shepherd on up the trail a ways who was new to the game. In fact this was to be his first day of shepherding the family's goats. The boy was probably twelve years old. Sobonathery had been talking to him the night before and trying to excite him about the job. But the boy was scared. Really scared. "Be sure to come by and see me in the morning," Sanjay had asked. "Promise you won't forget me - promise?" "I won't forget you," Sobonathry assured him. Early, early that very morning, just as the sun was peeking over the hill he was on the job leading his goats to their pasture.

"Would you like to come with me?" asked Sobonathry as he turned toward Ted for an answer.

"Sure would," answered Ted. "We'll go by the tent first and let Dad know where we'll be."

Sanjay had one of the closest—and richest jungle pastures in the area. We climbed the path enjoying the newness of the day. It was the time when the birds squabble over who found the seed first. Or perhaps it was, "Get off MY territory." Whatever their problem, Ted and I could have cared less. We were enjoying the day to the fullest. What could have been greater than to have Sobonathery with us telling us stories taken from his very own jungle village?

As we came closer to our destination all was quiet. The goats were grazing on the grass but where was Sanjay? We followed Sobonathery around some big boulders, and there we found him—hiding behind a thorn bush. At first Sanjay didn't see us, but as we came around a clump of jungle brush Sobonathry took from his sack a whistle and blew it loudly. It scared the already frightened boy. He sat down on a big stone, shaking—his legs visibly trembling. "What's the matter? Why so frightened?"

"It's the leopard. The leopard!" With that he put out his hands, holding them above the ground as he tried to show us just how big a cat it really was.

"He was just here! Just a minute ago. You scared him when you came." Sanjay picked up his batting stick and brushed himself off. "Please, Sobonarthy, please take me home. Don't leave me up here by myself. Please." Being the head man of the village, Sobanthery didn't want to contribute to the effeminate view of the young men of his village, so he took a moment to decide. Ted and I were anxious to help herd the goats so were hoping for a positive answer.

And sure enough, he did say "yes." We both found a good stick to help lead the goats with and listened to the lecture he gave to Sanjay on our way back to camp. The main topic we noted was to not be afraid. "You have a good strong stick. Put a lot of positive belief in it when you see a big cat, instead of running off in fear, come at him swinging with that stick, and hope that he will get the idea."

When we got to the tent Dad was surprised to see us leading the goats. In addition Sobonathry wanted a chat with Dad. He had decided that it would be a good thing for Dad to keep one of the goats and tie it up to a stump in front of the car—using it as bait for the leopard. This was all in the event that the leopard would choose the village for his supper that night. Dad agreed to the plan. A goat was chosen and tied up to the stump where the car lights would be focused on him.

Now Dad developed a plan of his own. Instead of sitting in the car and waiting for what may be hours until the leopard arrived, wouldn't it be fun for the kids to wait instead? If a hyena should come by first I'll just leave a gun to fit him, but in case of a leopard or tiger first, they can just flash me out back by the tent, and I'll come running. Perfect! Perfect!

When the goats and men folk had left, Dad sat Ted and me down to listen to the plans that he had figured out. "Hey, man. What a plan! What a plan!" Ted was off and running. First things first! Ted wanted to be sure that he would have the right gun in case of a hyena coming first. He and Dad worked on that problem while I set the table for supper. I remember that Mosha had a delicious rice and curry supper that night, and we enjoyed it immensely.

The goat was bleating big time when Dad asked if we had all we needed in the car for the evening. Dad had set the timing for us–Ted would start with the gun for a half hour. During this time he would watch closely for any movement out by the goat. If he saw a hyena or jackal he could shoot it and Dad would come running. However, were it a leopard or tiger we were to flash him with a flashlight and he would take care of it. I noticed that Dad had brought along a bottle of water and a couple of bananas in case we got too hungry. Dad set the noise level – tiptoeing and whispering. We passed by the end of the jungle hedge, skirted the side of the boulder hill, and there right in front of us was our car parked in front of the goat. That's the way it started–Ted in the driver's seat with the gun–I in the passenger's seat waiting for the gun.

Ted had the gun cocked to the right level. For some time we were amused watching the antics of the playful goat. He had found a couple of bones by the stump and was busy playing with them. When he would get slightly bored with the pace of life he would give out a few bleats and pull on his rope. In our whispered tone we would say, "Hey, Mr. Goat, get up and try some more. Bleat real loud and maybe the leopard will hear you." Finally the half hour had passed, and it was now my turn for the gun. The goat was still just playing with the bones. Ted didn't want to give up the gun but the more he protested, he knew that I would flash the light out back and Dad would have to come and settle the problem.

Ted and I were both good shots. Dad had made the rule that we could shoot hawks for they so decimate the area of good birds. Through this effort we had become fairly accurate in our shooting for there were many, many hawks in the area. My half hour turned out to be a pretty boring time. It was back again to Ted. And so it went – back and forth, back and forth.

"Hey, Sis, I am soooo sleepy. Can't stay awake." Ted stretched out in his seat and yawned. Soon he was gone–sound asleep. Now it was my turn. I soon found that no way could I stay awake either. So I decided to call it a day and signal for Dad to come and get us. With that I fell asleep and suddenly was awakened with, "June.....June, don't you want to get the hyena?"

Pulling myself together I looked out at the goat and sure enough there was a hyena chewing on the bones with the goat. He evidently heard the noise going on and trotted back toward the jungle. Dad quickly grabbed the door handle, opened the car door, and we took off on a run. We soon found out that we didn't stand a chance of catching up so we retreated to the car. Dad gathered things together and led us back to the tent and put us to bed.

Along about 2 o'clock that morning Dad awakened. As usual he picked up his flashlight and cast it about the campsite. There, just walking into Mosha's tent, was a huge leopard. Startled, it turned around, staring into the light. By the time Dad had crawled out from under the mosquito netting and picked up his gun the leopard was gone. Dad crept out of the hedge to the boulder hill and headed for the goat when he heard a distressed bleat. He knew what that meant. A number of big stones were separating him from the goat, who was now only a few feet away.

Ever so quietly he proceeded–crouching behind the boulders. Slowly. Slowly. When should he turn on the light? He didn't want to scare the leopard away, but he had to have the extra light to get a bead on his head. He could hear the jaws of the leopard grinding on the goat. Now must be the right time. He stretched up and peered over. The moonlight was just sufficient to get a good take on the location of the leopard. He clicked on the light, aimed and pulled the trigger. There followed a terrific roar. The leopard bounded probably twelve feet into the air and came down just behind some boulders nearby. All was quiet.

This was always an awkward time in the game. Is the cat waiting for the hunter to come and check him out? Or is he truly unable to function? Dad did not have the liberty of seeing him in his present condition so he decided not to gamble but retreat quietly to the tent. Early in the morning he would be able to check on him in a more safe situation.

My first realization of the new day was a crowd of men. There were men crowding each other in the campsite and men sitting on the boulder hill. What is all the excitement about, I wondered. Where was Dad? Where was Ted?

Slowly I crept out, trying to find my family, out of the hedge, around the edge of the hill, through the huge boulders. I came to a big group of men standing together all talking excitedly. Hey, there's Ted. And Dad. I ran to Ted and asked, "What's going on?"

Ted answered, "Look at your feet, Sis! That will tell you."

"Oh, Oh, Oh...my word. The leopard! Where did he come from?" Ted was enjoying seeing my discomfort. He let me remain in that state for a few moments. Then the truth came out. The size of that leopard was amazing. Dad had gotten him right in his jaw and now the village carver was beginning to skin him. All of the villagers were standing around awaiting their portion of the prize. Sobonaudery took hold of the situation by calling out to all of the men folk saying, "Everybody listen to what I am saying. Come this way and find a good seat on one of the boulders. I will ask the carver if we can move the leopard over to the hill, and every one of you can just calm down and see what is going on." Up went a hurrah, followed by a clapping of hands.

One by one they started jumping boulders and soon the whole hill side was covered with people. The carver and his men had dragged the leopard to the perfect spot where all could see. Practically every man in the village had heard and was awakened by the roar of the gun that night and was now out to celebrate the day.

Since the job of running Malapardu consisted not of working computers, barking Wall Street averages, or knowing the scale of the day's stocks, they can casually determine a day off. If something so portentous as happened the previous night took place—no question. But—no women help to celebrate the occasion. This is a man's job.

When the leopard's skin comes off, the carver cuts up his body into proportionate parts to match the number of people waiting for the treat. I was greatly honored to be chosen as the one to deliver the meat to the head of households. Whether it was a piece of tail or tongue, the villagers greatly appreciated every speck that they were given.

It was now getting to be late afternoon, and the folk were all getting ready to walk home. They had had a fantastic day off. Smoking. Telling stories. Throwing stones at targets. Just a lazy, happy day. I had been noticing a lot of hawks and buzzards flying around. They, of course, had smelled the scent of fresh meat and that was their drawing card. In my silly little psyche I had envisioned that Ted was getting all of the attention from these villagers and I was getting none. "No fair," I said to myself. "I can shoot just as good as he can. I can run just as fast as he can. Why don't I just show 'em that I can?"

The family's twenty-two rifle lay across Dad's cot as I ran into the tent. Suddenly the twenty-two and the hawk that I had just seen outside related to each other. That's it! I can show them! I can show them! From the tent pocket I took out the bullets I needed, filled the cartridge, and was on my way.

I found a boulder just beside the spot where they had been cleaning up the leopard, seated myself on it, and readied the gun for service. The men on the hill noticed my move and broke out clapping. This gave me some courage. I started searching for the hawk and in a moment saw it fly to a small tree about one hundred feet away. It landed on a branch and looked around. I took aim on him just as he decided to leave. Should I try to get him under the present circumstances—or just be safe and forget it all? The hawk was now up in the sky—some distance away when I decided to try. I took aim and pulled the trigger. I looked up to see the hawk flying away. Nothing happened. A big groan broke out among the men. My embarrassment was overwhelming.

I ducked my head and started to cry when I heard the groan start to change into a vibrant whistle mode. I looked up and they were all clapping. "Very good, Memsahb," they said, "The hawk just fell."

Mosha, who was working on some supper, came out from the cook tent and told me how proud he was of me. That made me so happy I ran to the tent, picked up Ketchup, and shared with her all of the day's excitements.

June and Ted with the leopard

~ twenty-three ~

First Day of School

He stood up and explained to the room that what I had done was worthy of a much greater punishment, but that he would suffice it for me to be tied up for the rest of the day.

The weather was getting hotter and sultrier by the day. Tommy Tucker was spending more and more time in his box where a very slight movement of air came through his window. If he didn't need a drink he still chose Dad's shirt to sleep in. Otherwise, along about noon, during the real heat of the day, he would leave his friends out in the trees, come on down the roof, and slide into his home cage. First he would take some gulps of fresh water that Mosha had left for him then would spread eagle on the floor totally content with life in general.

The debilitating heat announced to all that the time for hill leave had arrived. Every year the mission gave the women and children of the group two months to help avoid the paralyzing effect of the tropical heat. The men folk were able only to escape the intense heat for 6 weeks—a timeline that did not disrupt the train of endeavors. During this time the native workers would take over and do a great job. Why is it that they could face the heat and we, the white people, couldn't? When this is all that they have known—grown up with in fact—they only see it as a minor inconvenience.

A derzzi man had been to our house now for a few days. He had been sewing up a storm, shirts and shorts for Ted and Dad and dresses for me and Mom. Mom had gone to the bazaar a few times, picking out some fairly pretty fabrics for the clothes and drawing pictures of how she wanted them sewn.

This summer we had chosen to go to Missouri—a village up in the Himalayas. At this village there was a Christian school—1st to 12th grade. Built on the side of a mountain it was perhaps four or five miles from the village. Missouri was a favorite summer vacation spot for many of the foreigners living in India. Spread out in this vicinity was a number of little homes built for these foreigners to rent. We and the Coynes had chosen a couple of cabins just above the school perhaps a mile or so away.

The day finally came when we had to say good-bye to our dads and Tommy and be on our way. Mrs. Coyne and her children were in the same train car as we, which made it great for the four of us kids. Day and night the train would whistle loudly then roll to a stop at a village train station. There it would sit for perhaps five or ten minutes, whistle loudly again, and pull out for another village on down the tracks.

Stopping at these stations along the way was our means of getting fresh food. At meal time we would look for a man on the station platform selling pecoras, chappatis, bananas, or mangoes, etc. One time we stopped for a few minutes and bought some food along with a stack of bananas. Ted and I were so hungry we pulled off a banana each, sat down, and zipped off the peelings. Ted sat by the window and was peacefully chewing his prize banana when we saw a monkey sneaking down from the roof of the car. Coming from behind Ted, he had his eye on the banana, and just at the right moment reached in and grabbed it out of his hand. Ted let out a roar and jumped to grab it back. Too late. The monkey was already back on top of the car with his buddies enjoying the feast.

Three long days and nights put us in Darradune, the gateway to the Himalayas. Taxi wallas were everywhere with every type of conveyance except for an automobile. There were no roads large enough for a car or bus so we all had to go up the mountains in a somewhat smaller rig. What appealed to our moms the most were the chairs carried by four men with poles over their shoulders. We can take turns with you kids they explained and that sounded wonderful to us.

Back and forth. Back and forth. It seemed it would never end. I was the first to give up. Then Punkie. What to do? Just about at that moment we thankfully saw a taxi man team coming down the trail with no customers attached! Would they take on another group? Even though you have already made the trip once today? Please. Please. They agreed and on hopped Punkie and me. We shared our ride with the boys and our moms shared theirs together.

We found our house to be cold and bare. But soon it was supplied with curtains--the bathroom and kitchen were given fillers, and we soon had a blazing fire in the stove. This place was built right on the side of a mountain with a little trail going down the bare edge to the school, probably about a mile away. From our windows we could look out upon a beautiful sight. From our vantage point high up on the mountainside we could look out over the vast plains of India, lying at our feet.

***

Monday was to be the big day, the starting of our first day of school. From a suitcase I took out my favorite new dress. It was so pretty with a navy skirt and a white top, with bright red stripes ringing the skirt. Punkie chose one with the same colors that looked very patriotic. Our moms instructed the boys not to leave us, either going or coming. We kissed them good-bye, and we were on our way.

Mr. Emmer was our teacher. We had met him the day before, and he did seem like a caring young man. Good looking. Dressed nicely. We had been told that he was from England and had a very heavy British accent. And now as we came into the classroom he was busy assigning seats. My heart was pounding so fast and hard. I tried to hide the fact and not let him know, but I'm afraid my stumbling around gave my secret away.

On the way into the school I had kicked a pretty red stone and decided that it was too pretty to just leave out on the playground so I turned around and picked it up. And now our teacher was giving us a nice but very stern welcome. I quietly fished in my school bag for the stone and started playing with it on the top of my desk...when Mr. Emmer stopped his talking. Silence. More silence.

In a moment I glanced up to see why the talking had stopped. Mr. Emmer was staring at me—and not just a passive stare but a deep riveting stare. Silence! Still silence. After what seemed an eternity he said, "Miss Flaiz, what are you playing with?"

"Well, it's just a stone."

"Do you think that a little stone is as important to play with as it would be listening to your teacher speaking to you?" His staring eyes were directed coldly at me.

"I'm waiting for an answer," he said.

I was aware that all of the children in the room were turned and watching me.

I was struck dumb and simply couldn't say a word.

"Miss Flaiz, I want you to take that little stone to the door and throw it out on the playground. We will wait for you before we continue." Slowly I got up and walked in front of all those children. Quickly the tears came and soon I was dissolved into crying.

It was two days later when the teacher announced that we would be writing a letter that day to our grandpa and grandmas wherever that may be. I was excited. I jumped up and ran two aisles over to Ted to ask him for our grandparent's address. It was, of course, against the rules of the school to get up without permission and walk around in the room. But coming from my jungle background it seemed perfectly normal.

Mr. Emmer got out of his chair and left for the cafeteria. There he procured a large dish cloth and came back in without my noticing his departure. He knelt down beside me, took a hold of my left leg and tied it to the leg of the desk. "Oh my goodness! What have I done now?" He stood up and explained to the room that what I had done was worthy of a much greater punishment but that he would suffice it for me to be tied up for the rest of the day.

My Mom explained to me that night that in England, where Mr. Emmer came from, their ideas of punishment for children were quite severe and that I must not judge all of school by what I experienced there.

In fairness to Mr. Emmer, I would like to say that many years later my husband and children and I were on our way to the mission field when we stopped by a large church to take in the services there. It happened to be Mr. and Mrs. Emmer's local church and some mutual friends got us together. Mr. Emmer told me that day, "Ever since our days in Missouri I have prayed to the Lord that our paths would cross again so that I could have the opportunity of apologizing to you for the way I treated you in school. I was so new in teaching and had been taught that I must be very severe in dealing with punishment and young children so that they will grow up knowing the importance of rules. I am so very very sorry. Do you think that at this late date you could find it in your heart to forgive me?" I assured him that he had been forgiven many years before.

~ twenty-four ~

The Cave

"It can't be.......but it is. A leopard!"

"G' mornin', Mrs. Coyne, just need to talk to Freddie for a minute." Ted took off his cap as he spoke to Freddie's mother.

"Sure. Come on in. Don't believe he's awake yet," said Mrs. Coyne as she led the way to his bedroom. Sure enough. They found Freddie sound asleep snoring through a dream.

"Hey, you lazy bum. Did you forget that today's Sunday and that we're going out to shoot hawks today?" Freddie awoke with a start. "I'll be with you in.....in.....let's see–a half hour. How's that?"

"See you then," said Ted, adding, "Hey, I'm out of ammunition. I will have to pick up some rocks to fit my sling shot on the south side of the house." And with that he was on his way home.

What a beautiful day it was. Sun shining. Birds singing. Bees humming. "It looks like Osman brought his goats over for the day," said Ted to himself as he took in the beauty of the scene. It was such a clear day he could see forever. Darra Dune at the foot of the mountain. Beyond? Empty fields here and there with rich jungle land. And beyond that– the same until it all seemed to mesh into a gentle purple bordering the curve of the earth. A timid nudge against his knee brought him back to reality. One of Osman's goats was asking for an ear rub. "Here you go fellow," said Ted as he rubbed his ears and neck. All of the goats were equipped with a little bell attached to a string around their necks. Should one of the goats wander off into the jungle this would help the shepherd to find him again.

Ted loved the tinkling sound they made and so encouraged Osman to bring his goats to graze at any time. This he did quite often.

"My ammunition bag! Anyone seen my ammunition bag!?" Ted was yelling through the house.

"Have you looked on the back porch?" I asked, half asleep. Sure enough, there he found it—thrown to the side.

"I wish people would be more careful where they put things," groused Ted forgetting yesterday completely—throwing it there while he laced up his shoes. And now when he picked up his bag, he looked inside and found only two little stones.

"Wow, it's going to take awhile to fill this up again."

And there he was when Freddie found him on the rock slide behind the house. "Have a great time, guys. And be careful, remember just hawks. No good birds," cautioned Dad as they started on their trek.

The path to the school looked inviting, and yes, there were hawks on the trail. They had seen them many times on their way to and coming from school. On the way down the hill they passed the mouth of a cave. It looked so intriguing and how they did want to go in and look around. But Mom and Dad had cautioned them to never go in for it could easily spell disaster. No one knew what a cave held—drop-offs of hundreds of feet? Inner nets connecting each other that could easily confuse a person to lose his way? Snakes? Other animals? So everyday when passing this cave they had to mentally suppress the desire to go in and look around. But now????

"Just stick our heads in?"

"Dad and Mom would sure understand that."

"Like this?" To help Freddie realize what he meant, Ted stuck his head in and looked around. "Oh. My goodness. This is really something." In a moment he had forgotten all about Mom and Dad and was stalking around the entrance to the cave. Freddie followed him in. It took a minute for their eyes to adjust to the darkness.

"Hey, there's another entrance to this cave. Look. See. Up there.'" Ted was pointing to a spot of light coming down from above. Sure enough. And.....and.....What's that..... just this side of the entrance? "It can't be.......but it is. A leopard! A LEOPARD!" Ted was whispering to Freddie as his eyes adjusted to the darkness. Freddie stood paralyzed with fright, facing the leopard which was only about ten or twelve feet away from him. The leopard was taking in the situation as he sat motionless except for his tail twitching slowly back and forth. He was intently watching every motion of the boys.

"Let's get out of here," said Ted. Turning, he stumbled over some big boulders, picked himself up, and continued. Freddie was having some difficulties of his own, but in a moment they both exited the cave and in so doing drank in the sweet feeling of safety that distance gives.

Faster than ever before they climbed the hill toward home. A small pebble rolled down the trail alerting them to the fact that someone was coming. And imagine their surprise to see Dad with his big gun coming around a bend in the path.

Dad stopped momentarily. "I'm looking for a leopard. He just killed one of Omada's goats." Ted looked at Freddie, and they both just shrugged their shoulders.

"See you later," said Dad as he passed them by.

On their way home Ted and Freddie tried to excuse their apparent dishonesty. "I just couldn't....just couldn't....tell Dad that I'd disobeyed him and had gone into that cave. Someday I'll make it right."

And he did. For one day—years later he told the story to Dad. However, it was with a certain sense of reverence and awe that they passed that very spot every day on their way to and from school.

~ twenty-five ~

Ouch! It Hurts

" June, I'd like to bump into you again some time. But maybe not just like this. O.K?"

In the game yard to the school there were some swings that had been built up. They were pretty high as they took in all of the school not just the younger children. One day I had the chance of swinging to my heart's content. At home Dad had fixed some good swings in the mango trees. These had given Ted and me some good experience in swinging and doing some fancy tricks at the same time. On this particular day I was showing off all that I had learned. I was secretly pleased with the audience that I had, but was much too shy to admit it to anyone. I decided that I would pump up high, sitting on my hands.

With that I let go of the ropes and was working up a pretty high swing when suddenly the seat flipped over sending me through the air upside down and groping for the ropes.

What a deal! Now I was wishing for no audience at all. But instead I heard people calling all over, "Come and see! Come and see!"

"Ouch! Ouch," I cried as one of the teachers was examining me for any fractures. Soon there was a big crowd surveying every move I made. The teacher picked up my left hand very carefully and Oh, Oh, Oh, it was sooooooo painful. The school nurse was called, and it was decided, on the spot, that it was a broken arm. She very carefully wrapped it in a splint and explained to Ted and Freddie that they needed to help me, one on each side, all the way home. We made it!

Mother insisted the next day that I stay at home and rest my arm. It didn't take a lot of persuasive ability on Mom's part to talk me into it. However on the following day when I wanted so much to stay at home, I decided on a plan. If I string a line to Mom just maybe, JUST MAYBE she will fall for it. With a real sorrowful expression, I said in a whisper, "I feel so edgy, Mom. How long do you think I have to live?" Mom got on her knowing smile. She wasn't taken in by all the pathos. And off to school I went.

Exactly one month later Freddie, Ted, Punkie, and I were playing tag on the hillside beside our house. There was a great tree on the grounds there that was special to climb. In our plays and stories we would use this tree to fashion our escapes or perhaps our lookout from the mast of our sail boat. However on this particular day we were just playing tag. Freddie had been caught and was in an escape mode. He quickly shimmied up the tree and took the long lateral first branch out figuring that no one would be foolish enough to follow. It was obvious that the branch couldn't hold two people. But it did. I followed him out, out to the very end, when we heard a CRACK and down it went. When we landed on the ground I was on the bottom—my left arm underneath me, the branch next, and Freddie on top. Next followed a trip into town to see a doctor who had an x ray machine. The diagnosis? A break just one inch from the original one.

Flat land anywhere near the school was in real scarcity. Rock walls were built in many places in an effort to keep the children away from danger. Just to the south of the school was a frightening cliff—perhaps a few hundred feet down. A strong rock wall had been built on the edge, and the children had been warned not to ever, ever cross over. One day Ted and Freddie were talking to some boys by the wall when Roger came up. He told them that he had just seen a lizard go over the stone wall, and he had to go over quick and recover it. The boys were shocked and told him that he would be in deep trouble if he did and if any of the faculty found out. No problem. He had to go right now.

Quickly he climbed over the wall and began looking for the lizard. There was about two feet of shelf before the cliff fell away. He was standing on a rock—just on the edge when the boys saw it give away. Roger tried desperately to grab the wall but couldn't reach it. He then tried to catch onto a bush nearby, but it was too far away. He called for help as his support was giving away, but the boys could do nothing. Down. Down. They could hear him screaming all the way. Then quiet.

The faculty got together a rock climbing group. Together they climbed down and around the cliff and found that Roger had not survived the fall. It was a heart breaking message that they had to send to his folks. The family decided that they wanted him to be buried up on the mountain side. I shall always remember the sadness of that day, and especially the moment that we all sang together the song, "Oh we see the gleams of the golden morning piercing through this night of gloom. Oh, we see the gleams of the golden morning that will burst the tomb."

The day that Dad and Dr. Coyne got there was a real joy. There was so much to tell him and to share with him. I had to tell him about all of the kids in my room and also about some of the older ones that had taken my attention. “Like who?” Dad asked.

“Like Keith White,” Mom said.

“Now who is Keith White?” asked Dad.

“Oh, just a nice boy. He’s in the seventh grade.”

“In the seventh grade, huh? How did you get acquainted with him?”

“It’s kind of a long story. Not interesting,” I said as I started to leave the living room.

“Hey, hey,” said Dad. “I want to hear how you got acquainted with this Keith fellow.”

“Well.....well..... O.K. You see I was at school one day when I saw a clock and noticed that I was late to the next class. So I hurried up—fast as I could go, and when I was coming around a corner I ran into Keith. It knocked me down. Keith was so nice; he picked me up and brushed off my dress all the time telling me such nice things.”

“Like what?” asked Dad.

“Well.....like.....this dress I have on. All of the time he was brushing me off he was saying what a pretty dress it was. The white lace, the ruffles, the color. And when he got through cleaning me up he said something like, “O.K., June, I’d like to bump into you again some time. But maybe not just like this. O.K?”

“How nice,” said Dad. “It sounds like we have some real gentlemen in this school.”

"That we do," added Mom. "Before this happened I could hardly get June to ever wear this dress. She just didn't like it. Now I can't get her out of it."

Our time in the Himalayas went by in a whiz and now it was time to say good-bye. We had made some friends, but it was time to get home to Tommy Tucker, our pigeon friends, Mosha, and others.

~ twenty-six ~

Oozu's Problem

I turned to the audience awaiting my triumph—
when I saw the expressions on their faces.
They were horrified...

It was a bright sunny morning when Oozu appeared at the back door one day. Mom and Dad had already gone to work so Mosha had brushed him off onto me.

"Memsahb, I have some poor news," he said.

"Why, Oozu, what's wrong?"

"Do you remember the chickens you gave us money for?"

"Yeah, I think so."

'Well, we are out of money. We can't get them any food. So now they can't make any eggs. It's very sad."

"How much do you need?"

"About five rupees."

"Ouch. That's too much for me to give you. Come back tomorrow morning—early—and Dad will give you what you need."

Oozu appeared bright and early the next day, and Dad rewarded him with the money. He took off with a spring in his step and a whistle on his lips. That started me to thinking.

Why should he get something for nothing? He's going to make a lot of money on those five rupees. Just think of all the eggs he can sell because of the money Dad gave him. He should have to work for it. I piously finished dressing Ketchup for the day and placed her on my bed. I didn't want to give the problem to Mom and Dad. They were always so busy. I'll just take care of it myself.

Tommy Tucker came bounding across the backyard, jumped up onto my shorts, climbed up on my shoulder, and scratched around trying to get a comfortable place to lie down. Soon he was fast asleep—draped over my shoulder. This would last probably ten or fifteen minutes, and then he would go off to play with his friends in the mango grove.

I decided to sit down and weigh out this problem for Oozu. Brushing some stones off the porch, a plan started forming in my mind. Why not choose three stones—little stones—and have him swallow them? I had an allowance of thirty annas every week. I'll choose a bigger one, a medium-sized one, and a little one. If he can swallow the big one I'll give him fifteen annas. For the next one he'll get ten annas, and then for the little one five annas.

Great! This way he can earn that money. He can work for it! Just like Dad says, "Without work—no allowance."

Soon Tommy was sniffing around. His friends were in a nearby tree, wanting Tommy to join them. He gave a big jump to the ground, then bounded to the tree a few yards away. I set about to find just the right stones to greet Oozu with when he would arrive next week, eggs in hand.

I had been planning on greeting my family with the news about Oozu that evening, but somehow it didn't seem to fit all that great just then. I'll wait until tomorrow I decided. The days went by but none of them seemed the ideal time to explain the plan. Then one day I saw Oozu coming through the back hedge. He seemed a little cowed, but then to a certain degree, he always did and I gave it no more thought. I went to the kitchen, picked up the three chosen stones out of a drawer, and said brightly, "Good morning, Oozu, how are you feeling today?" He mumbled some reply and sat down on the porch.

"You know, Oozu, I have a great idea." Oozu's expression suddenly took on a bewildered look. "You want to make some money, Oozu? Easy, I mean really easy."

Oozu was a man of few words. In answer to the question, he nodded his head. "Alright...Alright," I said. "I make thirty annas a month and I have worked it out for you to get all of that." I laid down the three stones in a row. Then I put fifteen annas beside the larger stone, ten beside the medium stone, and five beside the small one. I then explained to him how EASY–EASY–it would be to earn all that money.

Oozu didn't look convinced. He swallowed deeply as he viewed the collection of stones. He picked up the smallest one rolled it in his fingers and asked for a glass of water. Mosha ran and got the water. With it in hand he put his head back and put the rock in his mouth. Down it went and with its passing a faint smile started to cross his face. He reached for the next stone and just as easily, it went down. Now the big one! Into his mouth it went. But.....but this one was different. Every time he would try to swallow it, he would gag and struggle and gag some more.

What if the stone got stuck in his throat and couldn't go up or down? The thought frightened me for a moment but was soon forgotten. Oozu kept on trying but in time had to give up.

But still it seemed best not to let Mom and Dad in on the plan. And Ted? If he knew Dad and Mom would know too.

So I decided to keep it to myself. It was fun watching Oozu earn his money and since it was for a good cause I chose to keep quiet.

The next week Oozu came and tried the stones. This time he was able to get them all down. Now came the temptation for me to choose bigger rocks so as to not let Oozu eat up all my allowance every week. The next few weeks Oozu had a hard time getting down the rocks. And it was especially exciting watching him gag and struggle with them. One day Ted happened to come running around the corner of the house when Oozu was working on one of the big ones.

"Hey, what's going on?" he asked, coming to a stop right in front of Oozu.

Oozu couldn't answer with his mouth full of rock. "Well, just thought it would be fun to see how big a rock he could swallow," I offered lamely.

I could see that Ted wasn't impressed with my answer. "Do Mom and Dad know about this?"

"No," I admitted.

"Well, they're sure going to."

And they did. I got a real "talking to" as they reminded me of what we were in India for. We had gone to India to show people what Jesus was like and this was certainly not what He would approve of. And so in tears and humility I signed off on the project.

In time things got a little boring, and I was looking for something to spark it up a bit. I could tell that Oozu was missing his allowance that he had been "earning." About that time a news magazine came to the folks from America.

On the front cover was a picture of a fight—a fight that had taken place between the two best fighters in America. The fight was to determine who was the best of the two. I was intrigued. If a fight is taking place in America and it's good enough to be pictured on the front of a magazine, it would certainly be O.K. to have a fight in far off India.

Again a plan started forming in my mind. How could I get Oozu into a fight that could help him somehow? I decided to offer him twenty annas if he would have a fight with me. Twenty annas was a lot of money, but still Mom and Dad probably wouldn't approve so I had better not let them in on the plan. We had four servants, and I decided to invite them to the fight. It would be held out back of the garage, a spot where we kept our wood for cooking. What a delight this would be. The servants —except for Mosha who had been in on the previous project—seemed curious and expectant of the show.

Finally egg day arrived. (Mother paid Oozu every month for the eggs and this was not a pay day.) I took Oozu out back to the scene of the fight and explained to him about the contest. I told him that we both would hit each other just as hard as we could and that way find out which one was the best fighter.

Poor Oozu. He had a hopeful, but not confident, look on his face. Soon the three servants and Mosha arrived and sat down. I had arranged some wood to form seats so they were fairly comfortable. Well, here we all were and it was time to start. Who was going to lead out in the procedure, I wondered. I guess it's me 'cause there's no other. What do we do to get started? Oh yeah, have prayer. They always start with prayer. "Let's bow our heads," I said.

"Mosha, will you start with prayer please?"

"No. I can't."

"Just a little short one. Please."

"No." It seemed a little strange for Mosha to defy me. But here we sat waiting for the program to start and since I had been the one to plan on it I decided that either it was me or no one. The last option sounded best and so I merely said, "We're going to see who the better fighter is– Oozu or me."

This close to the fight, Oozu now looked beat. How could he hit me–a white girl and a customer of his father's? The servants also looked askance, but said nothing. I brought Oozu to the front and positioned him just in front of me. His arms hung limply at his side. Instead of feeling sorry for him I was excited and ready to go. I jumped around a bit trying to get him in the mood. But nothing seemed to inspire him. Then I realized that this was an advantage for me and decided to go ahead. I drew back my right fist and with all my might hit him on the right side of his chin. Oozu was considerably larger than me. He fumbled a bit then fell over onto a pile of wood.

I turned to the "audience" awaiting my triumph–when I saw the expressions on their faces. They were horrified - jumping up to see if they could help Oozu. It was then that I realized what a gross thing I had done, remembering what my Dad had said to me in relation to the stones and Oozu.

It took awhile for Oozu to steady himself and be able to walk again without a wobble. I felt so badly that I emptied out my whole box of allowance money. It was special to me to see a smile come across Oozu's face again.

What I thought had been a great cover up turned out to be a sad play on my part. For one of the servants—I never found out which one—went to my parents with the story. With that I received another appropriate and logical "talking to" and a judgment call that prohibited me from going swimming for a whole week. And that was hard, believe me.

~ twenty-seven ~

Mom's Scream

"Thank you. Thank you. Yes, thank you. Thank you." Dad and Mom kept repeating themselves, until they were sure that the villagers got the message.

"Anyone wanting to go to Malapardu tomorrow meet me in the office." Dad was shouting into his megaphone, and he could be heard far and wide. Ted came running in with his sling shot hanging around his neck.

"What's up?" he asked.

I arrived about the same time with the same question.

"The village sent word to me this morning that two new leopards have moved into their area and have already started killing cattle." Dad continued straightening up his office. "The school meeting in Narsapur has been called off due to Mr. Christenson's illness. So I think I'll just take a few days off and catch up on my writing."

"When'll we go?" I asked

"First thing in the morning."

And with that deadline we all pitched in to make it work.

The next day all of the Malapardu folks were tickled to see us. The children crawled onto the car sitting on any open space they could find. The others followed along running just as fast as they could. We made quite a delegation – enough to scare any old leopard. When we came to our regular campsite Dad announced that we would be going on to a new location up the trail probably another mile– to a place just a little closer to the heart of the jungle. To get past the boulder hill we would have to clear a path around it. This took much of a day even with all of the help from the Malapardu men.

Ted and I were excited—trying out a new spot was always fun. Dad had already chosen the sight during his many hikes up the trail. Making camp—we all had our various jobs. Mosha chose his favorite spot. Then he would pitch his tent and all of the cooking gear. Now the family tent was another story. Mom, Dad and we kids pitched in on that. Everything was going smoothly when suddenly there was a scream. A terrible scream. Who was it? Who was it? I ran to the other end of the tent and saw Mom on the ground. She was writhing, holding her hand, and sobbing. "What happened, Mom? What happened?" Dad and Ted were there in a few seconds.

"I don't know, but the pain is so terrible I just can't stand it."

"Something must have bit you," said Dad as he quickly looked around the site. And then he called out excitedly, "Here it is! Here it is! A huge scorpion! It fell out of a fold in the tent. I'll kill it and get you some aspirin."

Mom was moaning and rubbing her hand. I looked at it and saw that it was beginning to swell. Ted and I were doing our best to try and help her, but we felt so helpless. With the aspirin Dad began to help solve the pain problem. But it continued so relentless that Mother couldn't sleep a minute that night. The next day it began to ease a little, and she was able to get a few winks of sleep the following night.

Nothing was heard from the leopards for the first three days, then the following afternoon one of the Malapardu kids came running into camp breathless. The leopard killed a cow up on the hill. It'll be coming back tonight. I only saw one leopard but there are two. I saw the tracks." He was so excited he could hardly get the words out. Dad stepped over to check on Mom's hand.

"Looks much better," he reported. "How's it feel?"

"I've almost forgotten about it," she answered with a chipper voice. "What can I do to help?"

Together they followed the boy up to the kill. They were hoping for an ideal set up where the killed animal would be near to a tree. Then they would climb the tree and wait for the leopard to return at sunset to claim his prize. "There's our tree," said Dad as he looked over the branches on the lower part of the tree. "It's too small but good enough. All of the greenery on the bottom half will hide us well." Ideal! Dad was comparing this set up to his two tiger shots–one had been ideal and one–not so good.

Back at camp they picked up the tree bed, flashlights, gun, and ammunition. And now quickly they hurried back to the site, opening up the bed and arranging all in order.

"Look at the sun, Ted, it's getting pretty low. We'd better be getting into the tree before the leopards get here."

"Right."

It was a beautiful night. The crickets were calling out their favorite songs. The night hawks were exchanging messages and the thousand little unintelligible jungle noises were making their voices heard. Mom and Dad tried hard to find a comfortable seat on the bed, but it was getting hard... and harder. Finally Mom decided that she had found a fair seat and Dad one too. And now started the wait.

Ted, Mosha, and I were back at camp awaiting the roar of the gun, which would tell us that the victim had at least been seen. One hour, two hours had slipped by. Many of the village people had joined us and were seated in the dark just outside of the tent. One of the buffalo shepherds was telling us a story–a story of when two tigers met at a kill and started a fight just right near him. Boom!.....Boom!

With that sound everyone gave a shout. The two villagers who had been chosen to carry the animal left on a run carrying the long pole between them. Mom and Dad were examining the leopard when they arrived. This was always a touchy procedure to go through for how can one be sure that he has not just been stunned by the shot? Or perhaps the leopard is mindful of the situation and will play a game with the hunter.

"Atcha. Atcha," shouted one of the villagers as he stretched out his arms encircling the whole scene. This was just too much to take in all at once!

"We only got the one but two came to claim the buffalo," explained Dad who was a tad bit disappointed. The men were excited and whistling up a storm as they tied the leopard's legs around the pole and carried him off.

Back at the tent Mosha was preparing a real tamasha. Every cooking kettle and every camping plate or bowl was being put into service. He first passed these out along with a silverware piece with which to beat the drums.

"Now when Thorogoda (the white man) gets here, just beat on the pans as hard as you can," Mosha told the villagers. "Let's just go through it once right now to see how it goes." As the villagers followed instructions the jungle exploded with noise.

"Wow! What a racquet. That is great," said Mosha. "When we see a flashlight back in the trees then we will start. Until then we will just sit and wait." It took only a few minutes until we saw the light through the trees. I'm sure there was never a king that received a more pompous (or noisy) heartfelt reception than this.

"Thank you. Thank you. Yes, thank you. Thank you." Dad and Mom kept repeating themselves, until they were sure that the villagers got the message.

~ twenty-eight ~

Peter in the Basket

He barely lifted the lid and
staring out at me were two frightened little eyes.

I opened my eyes slowly. It was a new day. I could tell that but who was talking? Mrs. Coyne? Mom?

"So what do you think? Should we go or forget all about it?"

"Well I wish that I could go too but since I can't I guess I will vote for you to go." In a moment I heard the front door slam and all was quiet. That was Mrs. Coyne—and where I wondered would she go, if she could.

Slowly I wondered off to sleep again and probably an hour later awakened with a bang. Ted was up and interviewing Mom.

"But Mom, Dad won't let you go without a guard—you know what I mean—a guy who will protect you from that rich Rajah. I forget his name, but you know who I mean."

"Yes, honey, I know. That will all be taken care of so don't you worry your little head about that." So much chatting had awakened me completely. I grabbed Ketchup and ran down the steps to where they had been talking. The only one I found was Ted.

"What's going on, Ted?"

"Settle down, Sis. Settle down. Well, Dad got home from Narsapur late last night. That was after you had gotten to sleep. I just couldn't sleep so joined them and that's how come I know." Ted explained to me how Dad had brought a letter from Narsapur—a letter from Mrs. Schutt to Mom.

Mrs. Schutt was a pretty girl—oh probably about twenty-five years old. Her husband was principal of the school in

Narsapur, and she was a nurse trying to keep up with the daily medical emergencies in the school area. The year before she and Mom had taken a trip to Madras to see if they could stir up any rupees (money) for their work among the poor. This letter was a repeat of that experience. Since they had been so successful she was anxious to try it again. And fortunately Mom was 'gung ho' too.

Mom reappeared and I quietly followed her into the living room where she was looking for her latest news magazine. In it she had seen some cute little up-to-date dresses which she liked very much. She found it, took it to a chair, sat down, and started reading. This was my chance, I figured. A really good chance.

"Mom," I said, "Mom, I was just wondering if just maybe...well, yeah....you know just maybe I could go to Madras with you. I know that it's asking an awful lot, but we could take Mosha with us and he could watch me. I promise I'd be good.....I mean really, really good this time. And if Mosha goes with us it would sorta give him a little vacation too. I remember hearing you and daddy say something about him needing a change of pace for awhile."

Mom didn't even wait to think about it. She just said, "Why, Sweetie. I think that might be a fun thing to do. Having you with me would be special. Yes! Us three girls together! How about that?"

The following two weeks were busy getting ready for this fabulous trip. In a short while the derzi arrived with his little hand held sewing machine. He laid it on the front porch and from his pocket held up his measuring tape. With that he took Mom's measurements and started cutting up some of her dress materials. These were precious irreplaceable materials, some even from Seattle! She would watch him for a minute then duck her head until she could stand to watch again.

"Watch it, Derzi. Watch it please. Don't cut it too ...too... big...Or...or too small.......Be soooo careful, Derzi.......Thank you, Derzi.......Thank you," and so it would go.

"It was interesting to note though, that as the years passed by Mom had such trust in her Derzi that she never again tried to direct him in his work.

Shortly after, Mom was checking on her dresses. It was the first time that I had noticed them, and I thought that they were really cute. I asked her if one of them was in a news magazine that we had just gotten from America.

"Yes," she said. "What do you think?"

"Great," I said. "I really loved that one on the front page, so I hope that you will wear it a lot. You'll look so pretty in that dress, everyone will want to give you money."

***

It was decided that Mosha would be going with us—and Rasham also. Rasham was a tall good looking young man, clean cut and close shaven. Dad wanted an impressive young man to watch over Jennie and Mable, and Rasham seemed to be the one. He was a good Christian and the son of the teacher at the school.

"How about your work, Rasham? Can you be away for about ten days?"

"I'm pretty sure that it will be all right." He and a friend owned a rickshaw and were trying to raise enough money to buy a second one. The friend agreed and would be happy to take over for ten days.

"Now Rasham I want you to go and have a good time, but I also want you to know just how serious a job it will be. You have heard of the Nyzam of Hyderabad. People say that he is the richest man in the world. And I also hear that he has watchmen in the three largest cities of India–looking out for the most beautiful girls of the world. If they are not guarded and then are caught they are taken to the Rajah's palace–and never seen again."

"Wow," (In Telegue). Rasham was sitting right on the edge of a chair, his eyes big. Terrified!

"Not long ago, one of these girls escaped from his palace, and she told the world what life was like in there," Dad was continuing, "you see, Rashem, the Nyzam gets very angry when one of the girls escapes. So when they recapture her they have all of the girls meet in a beautiful room. It is in the shape of a bowl and the seats go up the sides of the bowl." Dad held his hands up together showing Rasham the shape of the room. "In the center bottom is a stage with a table. There the girl is taken and slowly killed. This is staged so that none of the girls will be tempted to escape again. This way they know what will happen to them should they ever try."

When Punkie heard that I was getting to go on an "out of this world trip," someone had to pay. Her mother had to explain as best she could.

"We ordered that reading lesson from London to come for just that time, and you have to be here to take advantage of it. I'm sorry, Punkie, but you cannot go. Sorry, but that's it." It took some time for Punkie and me to get over the disappointment, but we eventually succeeded.

One night Dad took the five of us to the railroad station (thirteen miles away) all pumped and excited over the following excursion. It was too early to go to sleep so the passing of time fell to anyone who had a story to tell.

I can't remember any of the stories that were told—except for mine. I was dying to tell it because I had heard a number of people tell it a bunch of times. When the talking started to die down a bit I bravely started out.

"Well this story has to do with my Mom and her friend, Catheryn. Both of them had two kids—little kids. They were on the train heading for the mountains for our summer vacation. Dad would be coming later on. The train had stopped at a station. Mom and Catheryn had gotten us kids out, and the four of us started fighting over some fruit for sale. Just then they noticed two good looking British soldiers out on the station platform getting a little exercise. They were heading right their way. Mom straightens up, pats her hair into place, and says quite loudly, "You know, Catheryn, you really need to stop your kids from the habit of fighting so much." Catheryn straightens up, puts her hands on her hips, and says, "Oh really, Jennie...Did you forget that two of those fighting kids are yours?" The soldiers started laughing and Mom and Mable joined them. That was all.

"Thank you for that good story, Junie," offered Mable. "That's cute." I was hiding my face in embarrassment and then to alleviate that situation asked, "Isn't that the way people would tell the story, Mom?" "You bet it was, Honey. You did a great job." The train rattled on and soon all were asleep.

The following morning amid the train wheels screeching, the cars honking, and the people yelling, we were able to find a rickshaw which was capable of handling all five of us.

"Where do you want to go?" asked the driver.

"To the home of the Rajah of Teleprole. Do you know where that is?" asked Mom.

"Ah. Ah. Yes. Yes. I know very well." With that he started the pedals, and we were on our way. We had peddled for some time when a beautiful home appeared before us with a long park way out in front. The Rajah had explained to Mom and Dad that the guest house was for us, and the servants' part was attached to the back. It so outpaced us—we were amazed. The main home was only used by the Rajah and Rani when they were in town, but the guest house was just for extended family and family friends.

Mom, Mable, and I were excited over our digs. The bedrooms were beautiful. They had curtains that matched the bedspreads, all made up with sheets and blankets and fluffy pillows.

There were three bedrooms, all for our choosing. Mable took one, and Mom and I chose another. Mosha and Rasham were well served and happy.

Mom and Mabel slipped into their best outfits and were soon on their way. Dad had spent some time with Rasham drilling him as to just what he was to do on this trip. He was at all times to be aware of where the girls were and what they were doing—keeping them close together. He was to watch and be aware if there was anyone who might be eyeing them too closely or for that matter even following them. And as for Mosha, Dad told him that he was to be my "mother" at all times never letting me drift out of his sight.

It was still morning and Mosha decided that he wanted to see what the center of a big city would look like. Oh, but then he remembered that Dad had told him that he didn't want me in that heavy traffic—the city center. The girls had gone—and that left Mosha and me to plan our own day's activities.

"I can't take you into the city. Your Dad told me so." Mosha looked dejected.

"He didn't mean "ever". Let's go one time—just to take a look. He wouldn't care. Tell you what, Mosha. When we get home I will tell Dad that I talked you into taking me downtown once. I promise. How's that?"

"That's a promise?" "That's a promise!" And I kept it.

So with that assumption, Mosha went out on the street to flag down a rickshaw taxi. "Money," said Mosha. "I forgot money. I guess that we need money for the rickshaw. Hearing that, I flew into the guest house, opened my suitcase, and took out my allowance money. Fifteen rupees would be just about right for the trip and a little extra. So with that we were off. The closer we came to the center of town the more varied became the varieties of transportation. We saw buses, cars, camels, donkey carts, buffalo wagons, rickshaws of every kind and size.

It made for a melee and in this commotion a man with a basket came up to us. We were stopped at a point where a donkey cart and a bus were trying to pass. I asked the man what was in the basket. He barely lifted the lid and staring out at me were two frightened little eyes. I lifted the lid some more and fully exposed was a baby mongoose with a collar on his neck and a string attached to it. I closed the lid down tightly.

"How much?" I asked.

"Five rupees," he answered. I had just five rupees left and I handed it to him. Just then the traffic was breaking open, and he handed me the basket–the whole thing. What a thrill!

"Mosha. Mosha. Look. Look at what I have! A baby mongoose." I carefully lifted the lid. The rickshaw driver took a peek and said, "You won't have to worry about snakes anymore."

Mosha was positioning the basket so that he could see him better. "What shall I call him?" I asked. "Oh, let's call him Peter. I like the sound of it," answered Mosha. "Peter Mongoose." Peter sounded good to me too.

So that was what we called him—Peter.

Soon we turned around and headed home. Peter was grousing about the whole thing but Mosha and I were estatic. “I’ll ask Iwana if he has a box that we can put him in. And you’ll have to get some soft food too, Mosha,” I cautioned. “Cause you know that will make him feel at home.”

Iwana was a man that the Rajah had overseeing his establishment there. He was the only one who had a key to the place.

No one anywhere was as kind and helpful as Iwana, “Sure we can get you all set up in a few minutes.” And he did.

What were the girls going to say to this addition?

By the time they arrived Peter had settled down and all was cozy and quiet.

“Hey, Mom and Mable, come. Let me show you something.” With that introduction of Mom to Peter I could tell that it was getting off to a good start.

“Why, you sweet little thing,” said Mom as she cuddled Peter’s neck and back. “You’ll love our family. Yes, you will, even our Tommy.”

Oh. Oh. Another problem. How on earth will that turn out, I wondered.

The girls were quick to tell us about their day and the success that they had experienced. They were already looking forward to the next day and the experiences that it would bring.

I had mentioned to Mosha how much I would like to look around the big house sometime—just to get a feel of the place. And so the next day—shebang—it was open!

Peter had had a good breakfast and to my understanding seemed ready to go. With his collar and string on he was sniffing around examining all that he could find. I picked him up and toted him around. What a delightful home this was—the latest of every innovation that we could think of. After a little while as Iwana was showing Mosha and me around, Peter became restless. I decided that it was time to let him down. I tied the end of the string to the leg of a chair, and we took off without any impediments.

In about a half hour we decided to come back and see how Peter was doing. We hadn't heard a peep so decided that all was going nicely when we opened the door to the back porch and—and—Oh, no. It can't be. There was Peter's empty collar askew on the tile floor.

Peter, Peter, Where are you?

I looked behind the main wash tub. "Peter. Answer me. Where are you?" Still nothing.

"Where are you, Peter? How can I find you in this huge house?" As the tears came flooding Mosha tried to comfort.

"He has to be somewhere on this floor. He is too little to go upstairs." With that we started down at the end of the house going into every room calling, calling. Pretty soon we came to a big entryway with fancy double doors half opened. Iwana hadn't shown it to us on the tour. (It turned out to be a home theatre—with many chairs and a stage.)

"Peter. Peter. Are you here?"

"Eeek. Eeek." Quiet. More quiet.

"Peter."

"Eeek. Eeeeeeek."

"Mosha! That's gotta be him. That's gotta be him. Shine the flashlight over this way. No. No, this way." And sure enough. There was little Peter–half exposed and half hidden. I picked him up, gently carrying him to his little box and fixing some warm buffalo milk for him to drink. He actually gobbled it down, and soon he was sound asleep.

The next day Peter awakened to a lively day. I had put in two balls for Mosha and me to play catch with on the trip. I took Peter and Ketchup out onto the front parkway and chose cozy spots for them to stay in while Mosha and I practiced catch ball. I found a small rose bush to tie Peter to so they could "watch" as we practiced.

Finally we heard the bells of the rickshaw arriving. The "girls" we could tell had had a good day. Their smiles were big and their chatter – stimulating.

Even before they exited the rickshaw Mom said, "We arrived at this big building.

I was just over whelmed by its size. Huge. Anyway, we inquired as to the company that owned it and found that it was a rice and food shipping company to all of India." As she talked Mom was getting out of the rickshaw. "Should we go in to this place......or just skip it. We were kind of scared.

"You bet we were," added Mable.

"Well, we talked it over and over.....and over. Finally I said, 'Let's go.' We walked in and found ourselves in this beautiful big lobby. I went over to the man who seemed in charge and asked if we could talk to the president of the company." Mom was enjoying telling the story.

"The president? He's a busy man. Do you have an appointment?"

"No," I said. The man rubbed his forehead and looked askance.

"We don't let people in to see...Oh well...Pakkman, come over here and take these ladies up to the president's office." It turned out to be one of our best interviews.

"What was the president like?" I asked.

"He looked like he could be a really hard hitting boss, but to us he was like a bowl of jelly."

Mable told us that before they left he mentioned to them that when he looked up and saw these two pretty American girls he was overwhelmed. He couldn't do enough to please them." "Did he give you much?" I asked. "He was very, very generous."

The days whizzed by and soon we found ourselves again on the train. I was sitting by Mom – she had her arm around me. Peter was in his basket lying across my knees. "So did you have a good time, Honey–you and Mosha?"

"It was such a fun trip, Mom. I loved every bit of it."

There was at the train station in Nuzvid, a young man by the name of Sundara. He was a coolie but he was different from the others in that he couldn't speak. Despite the obstacles he was trusted and loved by all. When we came or went from the station Mom or Dad would give to Ted or me the buxshes (extra "thank you" money) for Sundara which we then would have the opportunity to do the presenting.

This time as we were coming into the Nuzvid station I was looking for Dad, Ted, and Sundra. Slowly....slowly.... slower and slower....screech.... screech.....s.....t.....o.....p!

"There they are! There they are! I see 'em. I see 'em!" I said all of this while grabbing Ketchup and the basket. Sundra came into the train cabin with his big smile grinning away. He stuck his hand out in order to give us a hearty welcome home. He also was trying to tell us how happy he was to see us coming to Nuzvid again with his grubbily gook talk. We, of course, knew what he was trying to say as he grabbed our suitcases and took them down the train stairs. There was Dad with his arms wide open ready to give us a big welcome home.

My eyes were on Ted. Did he see the basket? He ran to me and slowly raised the lid as he asked, "What you got there, Sis? Oh my word, it's a.......a ....well, I think it's a mongoose. Am I right?"

"Yeah, you are. And his name is Peter. Peter Mongoose."

Dad hugged me and handed me the buxses for Sundra. I always loved giving it to him 'cause it made him so happy. He took it and patted my back all the while trying to say thank you. With that we all piled into the car and headed for home.

The next introduction was to Tommy. Ted and I decided to keep Peter in the upstairs bedroom with us that night, get up early and before Tommy takes off for the day, let him meet Peter.

This we did—so very quiet. Tommy was still asleep though some of his early friends were already out on the roof top calling to him. We soon became aware of some movement in his box. Then he sat up and flipped his tail. We sat on some chairs watching. He seemed enthused over our being there and jumped from the window sill to join us. Which lap shall I sit on? First it was Ted—then me. Back and forth. Back and forth.

"Alright. Alright," said Ted. "Think I'll put Peter on the floor here beside me and drop Tommy down beside him, and we'll see what happens." Ted picked Tommy from off his lap and set him down directly in front of Peter. I hope they're not going to kill each other. For some time they sat there just looking at one another. Tommy was the first one to give way.

"Chirp. Chirp." Very softly.

"Chirp. Chirp." A tiny bit louder.

"Eerp. Eerp." That was Peter. Tommy was happily flipping his tail. They went in a circle, came together, and rubbed noses. That carried the scene—around and around they went—right on the kitchen floor, the best friends ever.

We kept Peter tied up in his collar and string for a number of months, then letting him out occasionally to enjoy the out of doors. Ted and I would bring in branches and even little trees to give him a feel for the outside. He seemed to enjoy having the floor of the kitchen as his yard. And just behind the food cupboard was his little nest that was warm, soft, and comfortable.

Every evening when Tommy would come home, before going to his box in the kitchen window, he would come down and scamper with Peter all over the kitchen floor. They would chase each other and "talk" about their day's activities. Then Tommy would flip his tail good night and climb into his home, look back at us, and he was off to sleep.

Peter was a dear little pet and lived with us for about a year. Then one morning...no Peter met us at the kitchen door. We called. We searched. We looked, but he never came back. Ted and I were broken hearted. Mom, bless her heart, took us to the upstairs bedroom and sat us down. When some of the crying had stopped, she had us blow our noses and said, "Just think of where Peter may be just now. Out in the jungle, he has found a friend. And together they are exploring the country having a wonderful time. Don't forget that we had the fun of his friendship for a long time. And now we have to give him back to the mongoose family and wish him happiness." In our minds, that talk helped us as we tried to always keep Peter in that pretty little setting.

~ twenty-nine ~

Den of Thieves

Dad had explained to us that if we heard someone coming down the trail, it would probably be good if the four of us just disappeared into the bush until they passed by.

"I've been thinking about Dungula a lot lately," said Dad the following afternoon. "Thinking about the family life there. Where do they get their water, their transportation? I think it would be so interesting to know a little more about them. Like right now—are they at home or on a raid?"

"Well," answered Ted. "Why don't we go up and find out?"

"Do you know what the people say about them—the people who really know them?" asked Dad.

"No. What?" asked Ted.

"They tell us to never, ever check on them for it will only bring sorrow and pain to us. And I'm inclined to believe them," said Dad as he sat by the fire whittling on a little stick.

Going to Dungala at this point seemed like one of the most remote things that he could ever imagine. In all of the years we had been coming to Molopardu, we had never seen someone we knew to be a Dungalite. The reason for this was because the village was sitting atop a mountain range and all of the villages that they raided were on the other side of the mountains. Malapardu was their friend, and they came for help only when in dire straits.

And so it was a sudden surprise when the next morning Dad announced that we would be hiking to Dungala that very day. We were going to find out the answers for ourselves. It determined for us an early departure for it was at least five or six miles away. "What outfit shall I put on Ketchup, Mom? She loves the denim one."

"That will be fine, Honey." I soon found it in my suitcase. We got together a bottle of water with some nuts and bananas and were on our way.

We had only gone a short distance when Dad stopped us in our tracks. "There are some things I need to talk to you kiddies about before we go any farther." He found a big boulder to sit on while he talked. And Mom found a seat right beside him. "When our family talks about Dungula we are usually doing it in a joking way. But I need to tell you that it is not a joking matter. They are truly outlaws and dangerous people. We are going to go to their village and hopefully they will be on a raid and will not see us. But should they see us we need to be very courteous and not act like we are suspicious of them in any way. Do you kids understand?"

"Yeah, I think so," said Ted. "If I bump into some kid can I show him my sling shot and show him how it works?"

"That would be fine, Buddy."

The sand on the trail was full of tracks. Dad had been teaching Ted and me who owned which track, and this trip was a splendid chance to see just how much we had learned. There were bear, hyena, pig, deer, leopard, tiger, and many more. Dad had explained to us that if we heard someone coming down the trail at quite a distance, it would probably be good if the four of us just disappeared into the bush until they passed by. So we were well aware of the possible dangers we might be facing.

On and on we trudged seeing a monkey now and then. They treated us as foreigners and scolded us loudly and clearly. Ketchup had gone the rounds—Mom, Dad, and me. Not Ted. He wouldn't carry her for any reward. To him it was sheer foolishness to bring along a doll on a scary trip like this.

"Hey, Mom, would this tree be a good place to leave Ketchup? There would be a lot of leaves to cover her up. And I will leave a bunch of rocks out in the path to remind us that this is where she is."

"Sure. Great," answered Mom.

I took from Dad's pocket a nice clean hankie and made a little bed in the crotch of the tree. There I placed Ketchup and kissed her good-bye assuring her that we would soon be back to get her. On and on we went.

Dad explained again that we hoped that these people would be on a raid and we wouldn't have to bump into them. However, if we did see some we could talk to them and there would be no problem. As we got nearer we could see signs of life here and there. The jungle was more cleared of brush and there were many more human tracks. We listened for voices, for any human sound. But none came. Finally we stepped into an opening and there just ahead were a number of neat little mud huts. They encircled a well which was readily used. Around the well were a number of chickens, scratching up their day's subsistence. And over behind one hut was a cowering dog.

"Here, puppy. Here, puppy. Come here, fellow, and show us your house." No go. He just hid behind another hut and peeked around its edge. This was it. They were obviously on a raid, but we were surprised that they took everybody with them, mothers, babies, children. The absence of people gave us a chance to look around, which we did with interest. We peeked into some of the huts to see what they were like. We found them to be just as we would expect any hut in another village to be. We got a fresh drink of water from their well and headed home (the tent). It had been a long hike and we were tired. Only one stop on the way and that was to pick up Ketchup, who surprisingly looked as chipper as she did when we last said good bye.

The next day it was "Good-bye, Malapardu." How we hated to leave and say good-bye to all of our little friends in the village. But knowing how often we came there we knew that it wouldn't be very long before another leopard or tiger would be bringing us back. So we could say truthfully to our friends, "We'll be seeing you soon."

~ *thirty* ~

The Castle

"This will always be MY picture of India."

Every fairy tale needs a part that says, "Don't believe me all the way." I'm thinking of castles, Princesses, the good fairy, and such. Now I shall tell you that part of the mystery realm of Nuzvid. There is a castle located just forty miles from Nuzvid that comes to us from the long ago–Dad said that he thought perhaps five to six hundred years ago. And from some of the people living there he had found out a few things about the castle. It had been built by a mogul–a man who had ruled that area of India for some time–-a Moslem. He had been overthrown by a Hindu man who was in charge for many, many years. Of course the conditions laid down by the Hindu prophets were but a stimulus to Dad who kept waiting for a good chance to investigate the place. And so it was that one day he announced, "Hey...anyone want to go and investigate the Kundipilli castle?" He was obviously suppressing his own excitement.

"Really truly, Dad. You're not kidding?"

"True blue." he said with a wry smile crossing his face.

"Oh, Dad, that's so exciting. Please. Please. Can the Coyne's go with us?" I was so excited just thinking of all the possibilities that could happen.

"Hold on, Puddin', Dr. Coyne and I are taking off four days next weekend, and we thought it might be good for them and us to just relax for a few days. We don't take time off very often you know."

"Oh. Goodie. Goodie. Gum drops! Punkie and Freddie are going too, going too! Punkie and Freddie are going too!"

The words were turning into a song as I ran out of the house to find Ted and share with him the big news.

It was decided to take Mosha and the Coyne's cook also. This would give the mothers a good chance to relax too, something they seldom had a chance to do.

We reached the village that housed the castle. It was located at the foot of a mountain range that comprised the beginning of a mountain group that spread out for many miles to the north. The jungle was quite dense in this area—lush and green. As we climbed the pathway up to the castle on steps made from slate rocks —intricately placed— we suddenly came beneath a large archway. Jutting out from the dense jungle, as it did, we seemed to be stepping over the line— separating today from the long ago.

Punkie was climbing right beside me. "Say Punkie, Now that we are in another time area—another country— you aren't just the same old Punkie anymore. You're now Princess Sylvia, and I'm—Let's see....Well who am I?"

"Why not Princess Jasmine? That's a good Princess name." And so it was—Jasmine and Sylvia. We kept on climbing as I started figuring out the plot. "Let's see. We'd be Princess cousins, waiting to be rescued. You see, we'd all come up here for just a little vacation when suddenly this Mondu, you know that awful old man who ruled 500 years ago—Goodness, he must be getting pretty old I'd say. Anyway when we stepped over that line back there we stepped into his kingdom."

"Wow," said Punkie. "Sounds serious."

"Look! Look!" shouted someone in the front. The castle!" I looked up to see the remains of what used to be a beautiful old building. A big circular section of the building met us in the front acting as a reception area. Rocks which used to make up the top of the castle were now strewn around below.

Looking around we found a stair step leading to the top of the circle. So much destruction. What a beautiful place it had once been. Stone arches, having fallen down interspersed here and there with wild colorful flowers and jungle trees. Further on we found two stairwells going down, down into the eternal black of night. From these holes came the flash of a bat, soon a hundred of them then a thousand. We had disturbed their daytime sleep.

"Look at their swimming pool," Freddie was shouting from beyond. "Can you believe it–a swimming pool at the very top of a mountain?" It took just about five minutes for us four kids to find our suitcases and our swimming gear and to be at the 'swimming pool' announcing our victory–that of being first!

And what a swimming pool it was. Beautiful with clear water, the sides being hedged in by huge boulders. The trail leading to it was introduced by a sandy path, filled with many, many sets of animal tracks. "Hey Guys, Look here," shouted Freddie again. He was kicking around some sand with his bare feet. "A bear track. Oops. And here's another one." When the folks saw the fun we were having, they decided to come and see what was going on. And in a matter of minutes, they too, were in the pool with us.

Ruins of jungle castle

Punkie and I realized shortly that Lilly and Ketchup were still in our suitcases, and here we were having such fun. Not fair, I decided. "We've got to go and get them."

"You know, Punkie, excuse me, I mean, your honor, Princess Sylvia, we need to make Ketchup and Lilly into Princesses. How do we do that?"

"Dunno," said Punkie. "Just say it I guess." And so it was done.

Sometime later we heard the cooks call out, "Dinner. Dinner." When we got back to the castle it was amazing to see just what the cook boys had accomplished through the afternoon. We built a fire that was enclosed by rocks, gathered a lot of wood to burn, put the army cots together, and made the beds. These were all lined up on the terrace of the castle, amid the broken down arches, jungle brush, and trees. "Looks to me like a house without a lid," laughed Ted as he looked across the expanse of a broken down building.

I found my cot right between Mom's and Punkie's. Dad and Dr. Coyne took the outside spaces and this gave the rest of us a feeling of protection. With all of the animals that had left their footprints on the sandy path nearby we were happy for all of the protection that we could get.

The following day we had the chance to explore the castle and the surrounding area. Like a magnet the swimming pool drew us to its cool waters, and we spent a lot of the day just swimming in its clear waters. That morning as we neared the pool, we were startled by a sudden eruption of wild voices—growling and angry. Ouch! How could anyone feel so bad toward us, I wondered? In just a moment I realized that it was the monkeys. The Daddy monkey came down out of a tree, picked up a good sized branch, ran to the pool's edge, and started whacking on a large rock. His mouth turned down. His eyes glaring. All the while he was being backed up with the ruckus of his family.

"What do we do now, Punkie—I mean Sylvia?"

"Don't act scared," she answered. "Let's just walk up like we owned the pool."

And that's what we did. The Dad monkey was the first to disappear, he with his family following quietly behind. We settled Ketchup and Lilly into some bushes very near to the pool—nearby just in case the monkeys decided that they owned the dolls instead of us.

From atop the mountain it seemed that we could see forever. Turning any which way we could look into the distance—see until the land turned to azure then softly—ever so softly blending into the blue of the Indian sky.

Looking to the west we watched as a train of many cars snaked through the jungle, its whistle barely audible from our space on the mountain top.

The following day Dad cast about to see if anyone was interested in a good hike. From the people of the jungle he had heard that north of the castle there were some hills mostly composed of large boulders wherein lived a family of tigers. They had found caves and had made them their home. And with all of the tiger tracks on the sandy trail that skirted the castle it was obvious that they were right. This was a situation, the likes of which Dad loved to explore.

Entrance to the castle

"You bet I'll go," responded Ted with obvious enthusiasm.

One by one they all fell into line—that is all except for the princesses. The hikers took along some food and water for the trip —

and with some sage advice to Punkie and me they were on their way.

And now–and now the day was ours! Punkie and I loved making up stories. The situation here was perfect for such–the castle itself giving to us a place to anchor these tales. The stories on this trip were built on the assumption that we were princesses, and we would get ourselves into some terrible scrapes. Getting us out of them was the name of the game.

"Let's see now, what shall we do first? Play stories, dolls or more swimming?"

The day before I had noticed a large opening in the fallen down rubble of the far side of the castle. It seemed to invite an investigation and I had determined that while there I would check it out.

"You know, Sylvia, I'd like to see what's inside that opening over there. Over by that tree," and I pointed it out to her.

"Yeah, me too." She was excited.

Fortified with our dolls and determination we started climbing over rocks–rocks strewn over the landscape into piles. As I started over one pile I spotted a small stone, picked it up, put it to my mouth, and started talking.

"Whatcha doin?" asked Punkie.

"Talkin' on the phone."

"A phone is a lot bigger than that," said Punkie. "I'll bet you've never ever even seen one."

"Have too seen one," I groused. "Seen one in America."

"Oh, that's right," said Punkie. "Wait a minute and I'll get you a real phone." She picked up Lilly and scampered across the terrace to the boy's woodpile, picked up a wood block which was just about the right size, brought it back and handed it to me. "So, who were you talking to just now?' asked Punkie.

"Well, I was talkin' to Hindu, the guy who hates Mondu. I was tellin' him that we needed to get home right away...... that we were in awful bad shape. You had broken your leg and I had broken my arm, and we needed to get to the hospital. He was tellin' me that Mondu was out of his kingdom just now, kidnapping kids. Will be back on Monday night. You better be gone by then!" "That's when we'll be leaving," I told him. "I can see the guards down there right now. Hope they'll be busy doing something else on Monday night. Something besides guarding that entrance."

"If I hear that anything has changed, I'll let you know right away," said Hindu. "I think that's so nice of him," said Punkie.

When the family returned from the 'tiger' hike, they were bushed and hungry too. Had they seen a tiger? No they hadn't gone into the caves, but they had seen many evidences of their near-by proximity. The boys decided that since it was night time for the tigers they were, no doubt, sound asleep inside their cozy dens. Time whizzed by so quickly and almost before we knew it Dad was announcing that it was time to go home the following day.

Punkie and I were the first ones up the following morning, and we quietly made our way out to the swimming pool. We noted that the monkeys were present (as usual) but inhabited a different tree–a big banyan tree just beside the lake. We took a swim but hated–so much– to say good-bye to 'our' swimming pool and castle.

"Let's go out on that big limb–there by the cliff–and tell the place good-bye from there,'" said Punkie. I recognized the limb to be the one that was each morning taken over by one of the monkey mammas. She would be sitting there taking in the sights of the day, no doubt pondering what that day might bring to her and to her family.

On this particular day I remember sitting in her place, on this coveted branch taking in the beautiful overview –the overview that the early morning would inevitably hand to us. I remember thinking–Surely there is no more beautiful a spot in all the whole world than what I have right here and because of that I must always remember every detail that is painted out there for me–the jungle at my feet, the birds, the monkeys, the spreading out of the mountains into the plains of the Indian west, and the endless jungles that go on and on to their inevitable blending with the sky. This–this picture will always be MY picture of India. Nobody can ever take it away from me. No one can ever destroy even one tiny detail of it 'cause it is painted in my heart-- forever.

But today it was Punkie and I that sat out on the limb, telling the place good-bye with all the kindnesses that we could think of. "Thank you for the swimming pool, the monkeys, the castle, and the sandy path with all of the animal tracks. We will try to come back at another time, but until then, Good-bye. We love you."

With that we trudged back to the castle. Looking down to the entry way I thought I saw some guards zealously watching for any passersby. I took out my phone from my bag and called Hindu. "The guards are there, Hindu, What can we do?"

"Don't worry," he said. "I will call and tell them that there is a village uprising to the north and that will be the end of the problem." And sure enough it was.

We were now on our way home—just past the rock entry way to the castle—the entry way to Mondu's kingdom. We had beaten him home and we were all safe. And with that the two princesses doffed their make believe crowns and settled back into the everyday routine of living.

~ thirty-one ~

That Tree is Moving

It didn't seem real but instead — it seemed to be part of a fairy tale — sparkling in the sun.

"In my heart there rings a melody—Jesus whispers sweet and low." Where am I? Where is the music coming from? I sat up in bed, rubbed my eyes. Ok. Now I remember. We were back in our old home in Narsapur. But why? Where was Tommy? And Ketchup?

I ran to the office where Mom was singing as she filed some papers. "Why, Mom, are we here in Narsapur? I kinda remember leaving Nuzvid but can't remember why."

"It's not surprising, Honey, 'cause you were such a sleepy little girl when we pulled out." Mom turned her chair to me and put me on her lap. "The missionaries who live here had to go to Poona for some kind of training and were to be gone for a week. They asked us if we would like to come and stay in their house. Dad decided last night that this would be a great time to come and catch up on his Narsapur work. So that's why we're here."

"But Ketchup. Where is she? Did I forget to bring her?"

"I stuck her in the back of your suitcase. You were just too sleepy to remember her."

I jumped off Mom's lap and ran to the bedroom, opened the suitcase, and there—smiling up at me was Ketchup.

"Junie. Junie. Come here a minute," Mom was calling.

"You didn't give me time to finish the story." Mom said this with a sly smile on her face. "Dad and I decided to take a little trip while we're over here. A trip that we dreamed about while living here—but just seemed never to have the time to take it."

"Where to Mom? Where? Tell me." Mom went on to explain that she and Dad had long had a desire to explore the ends of the canal–the canal that flowed in front of the house. We knew that it started at the Gadavari River–a huge river about thirty miles to the east of Narsapur and flowed down to its end in a large bay jutting into the coast. Mom straightened out her dress and put me on her lap again.

"Do you remember a family that lived just down the canal? They had a row boat that they rented out occasionally. Anyway Dad and I decided that we would take him up on it. We would make up a lunch and drift down to the bay and look around a bit. How does that sound?"

"Great! Wonderful! Where's Ted? I want to be first to tell him." And away I ran to find Ted.

It was decided that Thursday would be the ideal day. While Mom was busy getting the essentials ready for the trip, Ted and I were doing the same. When on a trip of any kind, Ted had a special bag that he tied around his waist. In it he kept his ammunition–rocks of various sizes. He kept his sling shot around his neck ready to rip off at any time he spied a target. Mostly his targets were just things that he would take a bead on, then say " Watch me hit it," and usually he would connect. But picking out the stones for the trip would usually take a long time. And me – my preparedness was always Ketchup. Now what would Ketchup like for this trip? And I would get out all of Ketchup's clothes and go over them one by one. I would finally decide on one outfit—only to reject it one or two times before leaving.

Finally Thursday arrived and all was ready—the lunch basket with all of the goodies therein, Ted's sling shot, Ketchup, and —my goodness, didn't she look nice with a bright spring dress and a hat to match. We each adjusted to the boat—the men folk to the front and Mom and I in back. And off we went. People walking along the canal road would be surprised to see white folks in a little boat and would call "Salaam. Salaam," and wave big time.

Going down the canal was truly pleasant—as we were going with the stream—no work to do. We waved to the passersby and sang with the minstrels—those going in the opposite direction. Ted and I thought it was such fun—surprising those in the boats we passed with a wave of the hand. As we neared the bay the seagulls came out in mass to welcome us. We took out of the food basket one chappati and shared it with them. They continued their welcome treatment—that is until they were sure that we had only that one chappati to share!

Coming out of the canal was quite a sight. The bay was like a big lake—surrounding the edges were a number of small villages. When looking toward the ocean one could see the waves crashing on the shore line. I noticed a patch of trees straight across the bay and up by the mouth of the inlet. Before picking up our four paddles to start our journey across the bay Dad asked us just where would we like to eat dinner.

"That jungle over there looks good to me," said Ted.

"Me too," I added.

"How about you, Mother? Sound O.K. to you?" Dad was asking.

"You bet. Let's go."

The water was great–calm and still. Dad designated who would pull and on which side. He handed me an oar and showed me what to do with it. Mom and Ted would pull on the right side and he and I would balance out with the left.

"What's wrong with that tree, Dad, the one over there?" I was trying to point out a tree to Dad–a tree in the jungle across the bay. It didn't seem real but instead–it seemed to be part of a fairy tale–sparkling in the sun. I took Dad's binoculars from his pocket and focused them on the tree. I couldn't believe what I was seeing. Thousands and thousands of sparkling lights and as I watched I saw that the lights were moving. How about the other trees? Were they filled with lights as this one was? No. They were just regular trees.

"Dad, you've just got to see this tree." I handed Dad the binoculars. We stopped momentarily while Dad adjusted the glasses. We waited for his assessment. Then..... "What on earth is going on? The tree is moving–actually moving. We've got to get over there and see what is going on..."

The four of us pitched in and rowed as fast as we could. As we neared the jungle we could begin to make out what it was that had so puzzled us. The big tree we found was covered–absolutely covered and crawling with crabs–tiny ones about an inch in diameter. There were literally thousands and thousands of them. One could hardly detect any part of the tree that wasn't covered by a crab. It seemed that half were making their way up the tree as half were coming down. Their shells were a light tan color and when the sun shone on it the reflection was magic–sparkling and clear. The tree grew in about three or four feet of water. In addition to the tree being covered with crabs, there were thousands of crabs in the water surrounding the tree trying to get onto it. And those on the tree were climbing over each other, pushing and shoving–all in an effort to hold onto the tree! We never found out what made that tree–that one tree–so choice to that army of crabs.

As we ate our lunch we watched the crabs fighting for a place on the trunk of the tree. Off they would fall only to get up and try again. Their persistence was remarkable.

On our way back to the house that day we stopped at the entrance to the canal. Lots of men were there waiting to be hired to pull the boats upstream. Dad chose four to help us. It was fun being on the boat where the music started instead of just listening to it from afar. Ted and I got to choose the songs and sing with the men until we fell asleep.

~ thirty-two ~

The Rajah's House

A clock chimed one o'clock and we headed for the dining room in our fancy clothes.

I was busy in the downstairs bedroom—busy dressing Ketchup for the day. "What would you like to wear today, Ketchup? Your sailor outfit? Or, Wow, it's going to be a hot one! How about your shorts and top? You think that would be good?" Suddenly I heard the ringing of some bells. Who could that be? Dropping Ketchup on the bed I ran to the window and looked out.

"Oh. Goody. Goody. It's the Rajah's elephants. Bet they've come to take us for a ride in the jungle." (In Indian lore a Rajah is to an Indian child or adult the same as a King or Queen. When the British took over the running of

Punkie and Junie elephant ride heading for the jungle out back

India they left the Rajahs to control their own people. The English just stepped in to take the top rung thus leaving the country with the least amount of disturbance. We were blessed in our area to have a Rajah who was always so kind and considerate.)

I ran out to ask the drivers what they had in mind. It's the Rajah's kids they said. "They want you to come to the palace and play with them for the day. One elephant for Freddie and Ted and one for Punkie and you." What fun! We'll be there. Quickly we asked Mom if we could go and of course the answer was yes.

It can be a trick getting onto an elephant. First one has to go through the rigors of crawling up on top of the lying down elephant, next take a hold of the loose skin and hold on tight because it can really stretch. When the driver tells the elephant to get up and jabs him with a javelin behind his ear, he can make the next move in a hurry. And depending on how hard you were holding onto his skin determines if you can stay on his back or not.

Butchi and Cuttanoma, Rajah's daughters

Cuttanama was the Rajah's oldest child–probably four or five years older than Ted. She was a lovely girl–gracious and polite but plain looking. Next was Butchie, a truly beautiful girl. Now Butchie was a fun loving energetic girl who loved the out of doors. And it was truly hard for her to accept the change of pace when her time came to accept the customs of her day. When she reached puberty she was not allowed to play outside any more. No more rough and tumble with us and so we were as broken by the rules as she was.

Lastly came Mova—the Rajah's only son. Mova was also a very polite boy, rather quiet and studious. He was a tall good looking boy, the same age as Ted. His life didn't change like his sister's did when he reached puberty for he could still swim, hike, and play games with the rest of us.

Play day at the palace
From top down: Cuttanama, Butchie, Punkie, June
Freddie, Mova (Rajah's son), Ted

The three of them were awaiting our arrival, and Butchie announced right off that they had a special surprise awaiting us. She grabbed my hand and led us toward the back of the palace. "Oh, oh I bet I can guess what the surprise is," I stammered. "A new movie, cause we're headed for the theater."

"You're right, Mary June. But you've never seen one so good as this one. You'll laugh your head off. Guaranteed!"

When we reached the theater Butchie explained that the mail had just brought a new flack of movies the previous day. Most of them were Charlie Chaplin films which she had already seen the night before. What a joy they were to watch with probably the most enthusiastic audience that they had ever had. From there they took us to the rooms and rooms of new clothing. It was like going to a clothes store where we outfitted ourselves in clothes that befitted the portrayal of any famous hero or heroine.

A clock chimed one o'clock and we headed for the dining room in our fancy clothes. There we met with the Rajah and Rani for lunch. And what a lunch it was. Our favorite rice and curry along with relishes and sweet breads of all kinds. But the crowner was the dessert...mango ice cream. The Rajah had just recently sent to England for an Icy Ball—the first of the real refrigerators. They were getting aquatinted with the menus of the western world.

The afternoon whizzed by and soon we were telling our hosts good- bye and thanks for a wonderful time. The Rani put together a box full of ice for each family, and we were off for home. Often when the elephants came to take us for a ride there would be a box full of ice to fill our water pitchers, and in the heat of the day what a treat that would be!

~ thirty-three ~

Jackals on the Hunt

*There were probably about twenty of them...
The smaller jackals were filling in behind the leader who was heading straight for Dad in a studied pensive mood.*

Many times in the heat of India, one's own direction would lead him to cross that of the scorpion or centipede. These creatures would avoid the dark cracks of a house or the crusty shade of a rock pile if the temperature was high enough. They would venture out of the shadows and would slowly browse around looking for their favorite eats such as a small frog, dragon fly, or spider. It was under such occasions as this that we would cross lanes and woe to us if we failed to see them first.

It had been a hot day and Dad intended to help relieve that situation by a nice drive to the jungle. Maybe the evening breeze would help to drive the heat away. Ted and I claimed our central seating places (Lying across the two front fenders) and away we went. In a few minutes we had reached the jungle and on came the search lights, looking for the big game.

"Shhh. Shhh," said Dad. "There are a bunch of wild boar digging for roots in the shale."

They turned their eyes to us and for that minute they were a dead red color. Then they went back again to their efforts with the roots. On we drove with the search lights sweeping back and forth across the width of the jungle. Soon the lights picked up some more eyes. Zeroing in on them we realized that it was a big pack of jackals. They started howling and soon picked up a real chorus like an explosion.

Dad turned the car motor off, and we sat in silence listening to the chorus of voices.

Soon Dad announced, "Think I'll go over a little ways and see how they'll treat me." Slowly and quietly he opened the door. With his flashlight, which he kept on them, he made his way in their direction. Soon they lost their interest in looking for clams and were concentrated on Dad. There were probably about twenty jackals and for a moment they froze—not moving an inch.

Then ever so slowly one of the big ones put a foot forward, followed by another—and then another. The smaller jackals were filling in behind the leader who was heading straight for Dad in a studied pensive mood. Without a gun Dad had no choice. He sprinted for the car and jumped in. Just in time.

The disappointment on the side of the jackals was evident. With their front feet they pawed at the ground and dog like—whined their disappointment. Those of us in the car were, to say the least, thankful for the outcome.

That night as we were getting on our night clothes in the downstairs bedroom we were busy talking about the experience we had just gone through when I heard Dad say in a surprised voice, "Hey, hey. What do we have here?"

We could just see in shadows as the only light was a wispy little lantern turned low in the opposite side of the room. Ted and I bounded over to Dad to see what was taking his attention. All we could make out was a dark glob of something in the very corner of the room. "Stay back," said Dad, "until we know what we have here."

Dad hurried to the lantern, turned it up to full strength and brought it over. In that first ray of light I saw a sight that brought on a case of shaking that I just couldn't stop. It was a huge, huge black scorpion. Ted and I had often found regular scorpions around our house. We would find them in dark corners, under a rock, or in the recesses of an old stump in the jungle. But nothing like this—in the privacy of our own home.

For some time we just stood back and watched it. It was hissing. We had no idea that a scorpion could make a noise. It knew that it had been found and started to get away. They are very slow and move meticulously. The bedroom wall was made of rock and slowly, very slowly he started to climb the wall hissing as he went. Dad dashed to the kitchen and grabbed a water pitcher. Bringing it back he put the open end over the scorpion and jiggled it a bit and kerplunk it fell back into the pitcher, just where he wanted it.

"This fellow is just too special to discard. Think I'll send him to the University of Madras. I feel certain that no one there has seen his equal."

With that he went to the car and got some petrol and poured it over the scorpion. The next day he found a can with a tight lid and shipped him off to the university. However before shipping him Dad measured him to be eleven inches long. He was very wide; however, I have forgotten that number.

In a few days Dad received a most appreciative note from the biology department head thanking him profusely for the "unbelievable specimen" that he had sent. No one there, he said, had ever seen a scorpion to match and it would indeed have a reserved place in their specimen lab.

One night a little later on Ted and I had gone to sleep in our upstairs bedroom. It had been an extraordinarily hot day. And on such an evening we would whisk the sheet off of our bed and lay it on the cold dark stone floor. I had called Punkie to wish her "good night," fixed Ketchup in her nightie, turned the lantern down low, and was off to a good night's sleep. And in that period-half asleep-half awake I felt something running over my leg. It quickly brought me to consciousness. I screamed, jumped up, and ran for the lantern to turn it to full strength.

By then Ted was up rubbing his eyes asking, "What's the matter, Sis? Better be good."

"Something big just ran over my leg." We grabbed the lantern and started looking for whatever it might be. In a moment we found him–a thirteen inch centipede. Mom and Dad arrived upstairs to see what all the fuss was about. Dad took the lantern and with the base cut the fellow in two. We then had two centipedes dancing around. The only thing left to do was to cut those in two and that gave us four. So we sat for a few minutes watching them all perform their death dance for us.

And speaking of death it seems as though it is not feared or dreaded here as it is in some countries. One morning Ted and I decided to take an early swim in the swimming pool between our house and the Coyne's house. It would be a good start in trying to keep cool for the day. We had gone only about a hundred feet behind our house, when Ted said, "Look, Sis, at what we've got here."

I hurried over to see what he was looking at. It turned out to be a man's head freshly chewed from his body. We didn't recognize him to be someone that we knew.

"Probably was buried yesterday and dug up by some hungry jackals," said Ted.

That was all..... and on we went.

~ thirty-four ~

Don't Feed the Bears!

What to do?
Should he make a big racket in an effort to scare the bears,
or should he quietly come to the rescue?

There was a camping spot that Ted and I loved. We would take Malapardu first any time but right behind it was the little village of Mondu. Snuggled into the deep jungle with a pretty little stream running along beside it—what more could one ask for? Mosha loved Mondu too, and he would take Ted and me for hikes into the deep jungle surrounding the village. Dad and Mom would care for the sick as best they could with just a limited supply of medicine, and then in the evening surrounding a campfire that Dad and Mosha had started, they would get out the Bible picture rolls and tell the people the stories of the Bible. Sometimes the folks would let Ted and me stay up through the meetings. The children of the village dearly loved this part of the day.

They would line up on the front row—no chairs, no blanket—just dirt ground. In the back light of the fire you could see their eager little faces taking in all of the excitement of the stories. They would laugh and clap their hands. Dad would give the drama all of the maximum play that he could rightfully give. So it was a fun time had by all. Before leaving an area, Dad and Mom would have a serious discussion with the people of the village about sending their children to the Narsapur school. Many came in answer to this invitation.

One morning I was out in the cook tent helping Mosha cut up the vegetables for the curry. Ted came by and since the folks were busy with the duties of the day, we decided to take a stroll down by the stream. Maybe we could catch sight of a deer—or even maybe a somber (elk like big deer). Mosha threw Ted a chapatti, saying, "Maybe you'll find someone who will like a bite of this." It was a beautiful day. There were a few jungle flowers sparkling up the woods, coming as they did from a monsoon downpour the week before. The trees were alive with the sound of birds and their music.

"Hush, Sis. Do you see him?"

"No. What?"

"The big black bear! Down by the falls."

"Hey, I see two."

And sure enough. There were two bears: one in the stream and one in the bushes beside the water. They were obviously looking for food. We just kept on walking and when they glanced up and saw us they didn't look startled or upset. Ted took the chapatti over to the bear in the bushes and tearing off a piece handed it to him. He took it and seemed to ask for more. Ted obliged but decided to share it with the other fellow. It was thankfully a large piece of bread, so he stood there for some time handing out the pieces.

In the meantime Mosha was at the tent working on the lunch plans when he suddenly remembered talking to the head man of Mondu the day before. This gentleman had mentioned the fact that a story was drifting around the village that there were a couple of bears taking up residence in the area. What, he wondered, would Ted and June do if they should come across such a scenario? And the more he thought about the possibility, the more concerned he became.

Heading down stream in the direction that he had recommended to us he stealthily made his way. Pretty soon he heard a commotion going on downstream. It was not a happy sound like birds enjoying themselves, but rather an alarmist sound. Mosha well knew this noise as he was akin to so many birds that lived in the area, and when they made contact with snakes or wild animals, they made the event well known.

When Mosha came around a corner of the stream his eyes fastened on a sight before him. He couldn't believe his eyes. Here were two children happily feeding two wild bears. Bears who would not give a thought of hauling off and swatting a person, much less a little one. What to do? Should he make a big racket in an effort to scare the bears, or should he quietly come to the rescue? '"While Mosha was trying to make a decision Ted was coming to the last of the chapatti. He handed the last bite to one of the bears, and when they saw that that was the end, they snorted and took off downstream.

"How lucky can you get," was Mosha's comment as he surprised the kids. "Only don't you ever, ever try it again. 'Cause next time it might not turn out so good."

"But they were such nice bears. I liked them," I said.

"Nice this time, but that doesn't mean that they would be so nice the next time." And so the incident was left at that.

~ thirty-five ~

Santa in the Tropics

That was sure nice of Santa.
Wish I could thank him.

The next day, Mom was tidying up the tent when she suddenly stood up straight and said to no one in particular, "You know, I do believe that tomorrow is Christmas day." She had to sit down to realize that she had for some time forgotten all about Christmas. Usually she tried to plan something special for that important day, but this time it had completely slipped by her.

When I heard Mom's announcement, I ran outside to find Ted and to tell him about the surprise. "You remember our Christmas in America, Ted? Remember how Harriet told us to hang up some big stockings and that Santa would put some presents in 'em? Remember? She told us that Santa went clear around the world filling stockings so he must come here too."

"Yeah. She sure did. That's neat. I remember we put up some stockings and Santa filled them, but we don't have any Christmas stockings in India." Ted's face fell with the last statement. He kicked the ground with his toe. What to do?

Now, as he stopped to ponder the subject, his face became brighter and brighter. "How about Dad? Why don't we ask if we can borrow two of his big socks? We'll get a couple of safety pins from Mom and pin 'em on the tent wall above our cots."

"Great thinking, Sis. But I wonder just how Santa will find us way out here in the jungle."

"No problem. Harriet said that he was magical and that takes care of it."

In a moment we were in to the tent looking for Dad's suitcase. "Aha! Here it is and in just one minute I will show you our Christmas stockings."

"O.K. kids. What's going on with you two?" It was Mom. With both of us talking at once it was hard for her to figure out just what our plan really was. However she did get the slant of what the safety pins would do and was soon looking intently for them.

She also wanted to have a little talk with Mosha. She told him how she would love to have a special Christmas Eve supper that night, but how can we make it special way out here in the jungle? That was the big question. "And, Mosha, we want you to have dinner with us tonight too. Can we plan on it?"

"Yes, ma'am, I will try." This was said with much appreciation and gratitude, but what a busy afternoon it presented to Mosha. By supper time he had a tasty curry ready, made special by the addition of some fresh roasted cashew nuts and raisins. For dessert he had cooked some sugarcane with the rice and topped it with some yummy mangos. We even had some special drink to go along—coconut milk. The family decided that this supper was pretty hard to beat. Mosha was greatly pleased and took pleasure in his ability to serve and to eat with the family at the same time.

That night, following family worship, Ted and I went to sleep with the stockings hanging just above our heads. We had prayed fervently during worship that evening that Santa would find us no matter where we might be.

"I have a problem," Ted whispered to me. "I just don't know how it can be taken care of."

"What's that?" I asked.

"Well, you see, Sis, I want a bicycle so bad. It just hurts. But how can Santa get a bicycle into a sock? He can't."

"I see. You do gotta a problem. Well, let's just see if... we.....can..........think............of..." and with that I was gone. Shhhh. How about Ted? Oh. Oh. There was a snore coming from his direction.

So now it was Mom's and Dad's turn to take over. "Mosha, you can come now."

"Are they asleep?" he asked in a loud whisper through the front opening of the tent. "They are and you can come in and wait here by the lantern." Mosha made an excellent baby sitter. He would often fall asleep while on duty, but the slightest sound would awaken him in a jiff.

Dad got out his powerful flashlight and together he and Mom headed for the village—a mile away. In a country like India, so near to the equator, the sun sets at around six and rises in the morning close to six. The villagers who have no electricity and are supplied with light from a lantern choose to save kerosene where they can and go to sleep with the sun. By six o'clock in the morning they have had a good night's sleep and are ready to go to work.

This particular night all of the folks of Mondo had turned off their lanterns and had gone to sleep. Fortunately Dad knew most of the people there. He whistled a long deep rather quiet tone and then called out a name. In a moment the person appeared at his hut door. Dad called another name and the same happened. Dad explained to these two men his problem and asked if there were anything that they just might have that would fit the bill. Both men were most helpful. One man suggested the possibility of putting into the sock sticks of sugar cane. He had some cane in his hut and said that he could have sticks cut up in a minute.

The other man said that he had a neighbor who that very afternoon had roasted up a bunch of peanuts. "And I know that he would be so happy to share some with you. You gave him some medicine yesterday that helped his little boy get rid of some worms and he wanted to pay you for that, but you wouldn't take anything."

Pretty soon the folks had their arms full of gifts, and they were on their way back to camp.

What fun they had stuffing the socks with surprises. Following such an exciting evening they both had trouble getting to sleep and anticipating the early morning when the children would awaken and see what Santa had left.

In the morning just about sun-up, Mom heard, "Hey, Ted, look! Santa was here. Look at the socks. They are full to the very top. Oh, this is soooo exciting." I was fighting with the mosquito netting trying to get to the socks, and Ted was rubbing his eyes not sure what was happening. Pretty soon it was all spread out on the cots—roasted peanuts, two cute little men carved from a bamboo branch, and sugar cane sticks.

"That was sure nice of Santa. Wish I could thank him." This was coming from me. My mouth was so full of sugar cane that I was having trouble getting the words out.

“We can thank him, Sis. Write him a letter. Can’t we, Mom?”

“That would be a nice thing to do. When we get home you can both work up a nice letter of thanks.

~ thirty-six ~

The Mystery Box

The trip to the station seemed ever so long. And then the box! There it was over in the corner of the room.

The distance between Punkie's and my homes was such that we could just hear each other when shouting fairly loud. And since Freddie and Ted and us girls went to sleep at about the same time it became a habit for us to call each other 'goodnight.' And since we had been together most of the day there really wasn't a lot to be said but 'goodnight.'

However on this particular night, when I heard the catching whistle I asked what was new.

"I have the most wonderful news, but I can't let you know until tomorrow what it is. It's something we've been hoping for, for an awful long time."

"Please. Please, Punkie. I promise not to tell anybody." All to no avail. What could it be? What could it be?

The next morning bright and early I was at Punkie's house. "O. K., Punkie. What is the surprise? I waited all night, and I can't wait another minute."

Punkie sat me in a chair and in a conspiratorial whisper said, "Mom told me this morning that it would be all right to tell you. Only she was afraid that if I told you, and it didn't work out, you would be hurt. You see, Junie, a hospital worker went to the train station yesterday to pick up some hospital things and saw a big box from England with all the children's names on it. His car wasn't big enough to carry it so my Mom was going to the station–(thirteen miles away)–to pick it up today. And what's more–all four of us kids can go with her."

What joy! What anticipation! What could it be–a big box with all our names on it? "I know what it is," said

Punkie with conviction spread all over her face. "We've been praying for ages for a bicycle, and I just know that God is answering our prayers."

"That's what I am betting on too," I said. "Guess the bicycle will be for all four of us. We can share and have so much fun!"

The trip to the station seemed ever so long. And then the box! There it was over in the corner of the room. "Hey, Mom, we need to open it now. Right now to see what it is." Freddie was urgent, but his Mom said that we would be home shortly. Again the guessing was front and center. What would we find? We arrived at Punkie's home, and the boys were out of the car in a flash. Freddie grabbed a knife and was ripping the box open.

"Hey, hey look. What did I tell you? A bicycle. It's a bicycle!" I was jumping up and down, clapping my hands. "But what is this other thing?" Freddie was struggling with the box covering. "Oh my goodness. It's another bicycle. And another. And another." Punkie and I were squealing with delight, and the boys were shaking their heads in disbelief.

Two larger cycles were blue and two smaller ones were red. Punkie's Mom wanted to know what the inside letter had to say. "Merry Christmas to Freddie, Theodore, Punkie, and June, with best wishes from The Rajah and Rani of Teleprole." How wonderful of them to do that for us," said a thoughtful Punkie.

It had taken quite some time for the package to reach Nuzvid. It was now well into February. But late or early meant little to the four of us. We were completely blown away. Every day the folks would try to get us to come in for supper, for worship, or to go to bed, "But please, Mom and Dad, just one half hour more. O.K., then just fifteen minutes longer. Please. Please, Dad. Please, Mom." And so it would go.

Prior to this time our days were usually taken over with swimming in one of the three swimming pools available to us. Actually these water holes were firstly meant for irrigation and secondly for swimming. The Rajah's cousin, Mr. Esha Roa, lived in a lovely home behind our house.

Surrounding his home was an orange grove for which he built a good sized swimming pool. From this he took the essential water to irrigate the orange trees. Mr. Roa's home along with the Coyne's and our home formed the outer edge of the village and beyond that was jungle.

Another one of these water holes was right between Punkie's house and ours. The third one was on the hospital grounds. So we had a nice choice. If one was out of order we could go to another. The Rajah was the builder of two of these facilities, and he chose to build at one end of the pool a stair-stepped high rise for us kids to have for diving.

Before diving in we would circle the pool looking for any centipedes or scorpions that might have fallen in. Even birds or bats would get caught in the water. After cleaning the pool of these intruders we would spend literally hours and hours jumping, diving, and floating in the cool waters. Beyond this we would develop games in which the four of us could play. We even played out stories that we had read.

Often, when we were swimming in his pool, Mr. Roa, the Rajah's cousin, would send his butler over to invite us kids to afternoon tea. How we loved that for he would have untold goodies awaiting our acceptance. Mr. Roa was a suave European-style gentleman: thoughtful, gentle, and kind. He loved telling stories, and we of course, were his favorite audience—in our swimming suits, dripping with water on his marble floor.

Ted, June, Mr. Roa (the Rajah's cousin), Punkie, Freddie

And so it was with a great deal of worry that we heard one day that he had gone away. Every day we hoped to hear that he had returned. Months went by.

Finally one of his staff told us a story. They did not know for sure where he had disappeared to, but—the story was leaking out. Leaking out that he had left for one of the holiest shrines in all of Hinduism—away up in the

Himalayan Mountains. Not only was he making his way to Amrinoth, but he had accepted the very "righteous" way of getting there, by lying down, getting up, and lying down again, just the length of his body. This was the way that he would reach his goal. This he believed would clear him of any sins he had committed through his life.

To me, in my childish reasoning, it seemed that it would surely take him the rest of his life to reach the holy place.

~ thirty-seven ~

Shiny Fur

When all was set, Freddie said, *"O.K., Ted. Do your stuff. One. Two. Three—GO."*

One day a Hindu gentleman came to Dad's office and asked if possibly his children would like to have a somber (elk) for a pet. His family had come across the animal when it was just a little fellow in the jungle behind our home. He grew fast and pretty soon outgrew their modest means to care for him. Loving animals as they did, they did not want any of their neighbors to kill it for food.

Ted and I were thrilled with the prospects of this elk, the size of a horse, but Dad wasn't convinced.

"You see, Dad, we can tie him to a mango tree, and he can eat all the grass around that tree, and then we can move him on to another. June and I can take care of his water and there you have it. O.K.? Please, Dad. Sis and I will do all the work."

Ted and I were excited. We could imagine that in a few weeks or months we would have him tamed like a horse, and we could ride him around the village. We didn't share that aspect with Dad but the rest sounded good.

The next day we went with Dad to get and bring him home. We fell in love with him the minute that we saw him and named him Shiny Fur. Beautiful, peaceful, and quite tame, he had lived with people for some time so was not afraid of a human being. Ted and I fixed him up to be quite comfortable, with plenty of water and grazing grass.

A few days later, Punkie and I were busy sewing up a storm in our tree house. We had heard that Dorothy Cormack would be there with her father in one week. Mr. Cormack was the president of our missionary group, and we, of course, wanted to show off Nuzvid. But Dorothy? How were Punkie and I going to entertain Dorothy for two whole days? TWO WHOLE DAYS! "Maybe we should make some new clothes for Lilly and Ketchup," said Punkie. Lilly was Punkie's doll—kinda beat up but still recognizable.

How can we talk to her for two days?" I said. "What can we talk about? What can we say? She will be so sooo... sooo...fist...ta ... Oh, you know what I'm trying to say, Punkie. Anyway she will be so proper 'cause she lives in a big Indian city with a bunch of white people. I know. She'll think we're just some jungle wallas."

Mother hearing of our crisis offered to cut out some material that we had on hand. She spent a whole morning fitting pieces to the dolls and then explaining to us how to sew them up. This we were doing when we heard, "Hey, Sis. Hey, Punkie. Where are you?"

"Sounds like Ted calling," said Punkie. "We're in the tree house," she shouted back. "What do you want?"

Ted answered but being so far away we didn't hear. "I'm tired of sewing," said Punkie. "Let's just go and see what they want." With that we scooted down the tree "stairs," and off to find the boys.

We spotted them leading Shiny Fur across a section of mango grove.

"We thought that you guys would like to see how well Shiny Fur performs. We're taking him over here by a special tree. One that has a low branch so Ted can get onto him," said Freddie.

While Freddie was trying to position him Ted climbed the tree and slid out onto the low lying branch. When all was set Freddie said, "O.K., Ted. Do your stuff. One. Two. Three–GO. "

With that Ted dropped square onto Shiny Fur's back. The connection lasted perhaps one fourth of a second, and he was gone–leaving Ted flat on the ground. Now we had a frightened somber on our hands. All four of us ended up chasing Shiny Fur over the mango grove trying to catch hold of his guiding rope. Once he hesitated a moment trying to decide which way to go. Freddie stepped on the end of it, and that was it. That was the first and last time we tried to tame him.

One morning we got up and looked out–but no Shiny Fur. How could that be? Ted and I ran out to see what could have happened. There was his guiding rope, tied to the tree–but the other end had lost its knot and its prisoner. We wondered for a long time just where could our dear friend be, finally deciding that probably he was out in the back jungle enjoying life with all of his family and old friends.

~ thirty-eight ~

The Tiger Hunt

The jungle exploded. Unbelievable.
Yelling, banging, whistling, car horns.
You name it—it was there.

"The Rajah is coming. The Rajah is coming." It was Mosha calling through the house. It was rather an infrequent occasion for the Rajah to come to our home for he usually came to the hospital when he wanted to see the folks. Dad had an office at both our home and the hospital. There was no such thing as a telephone so he could not call ahead and secure a time in which to come. Mosha wanted his employer to be in a receptive mood in which to receive the Rajah—giving us a moment in which to get prepared. Going ever so slowly, the Rajah's limousine was coming down the long driveway. The driver decided to park in the front of the house. Jumping out he helped the Rajah get out of the car and up the front steps.

"So nice to see you, Sir," said my Dad as he shook hands with the Rajah. "What brings you out so early in the morning?" Dad seated him in the living room along with Mom and himself.

The Rajah, it seems, was concerned about a situation that was arising in the vicinity. "So many people have been coming to me lately telling me that there are a couple of tigers that have moved into our area. And I was just wondering if you would join with me in seeing if we could get rid of them. I don't like to see my people suffering the loss of their cattle."

"Nor do I," added Dad. "What do you have in mind?"

The Rajah explained to him that he could call about one hundred men to come out and help them. "What we do is take hundreds of feet of cloth and string it out into a

V shape. Where the two sides converge we have a machan with hunters stationed. And then you see, Pastor, we divide up the group of men into two sides. They will have anything that makes a noise—tin cans, kettles, horns, musical instruments, etc. He went on to explain how the cloth will be spread out in the most likely area. Then the 'band' begins to play. Supposedly the tiger will be flushed out of his comfort zone and will be pushed to the center of the V. And at that time the hunters will take over.

"That sounds very likely to work," said Dad. "When do you propose that this take place?"

"How about tomorrow?" Ted and I were standing nearby taking it all in. The Rajah glanced up and seeing our pleading eyes smiled and said with a twinkle, "How would you kids like to help us out?"

Would we? WOULD WE? It seemed too good to believe. The Rajah sent his men out into the jungle to determine just where they should put the V cloth. Where had the tigers been seen lately? How were their tracks taken in relation to the area? Then there was the cow that needed to be gotten and tied to the stake at the convergence of the two sides. The lay-out for this occasion was a studied out plan—not a willy nilly set up where no outline was used. Early the next morning Ted and I went out to the sight with Dad.

The Rajah's men had found what they thought was a very good place for the V to be placed. At the center they had a special tree for the machans to be left—full of low branches and leaves. We watched as they put two machans into the tree. Actually these were two army cots opened up and spread out.

"They look so comfortable," I said to Ted. "We might even go to sleep up there."

We were all to meet on that spot at four o'clock. The one hundred men had done this many times and knew to be quiet. They were placed at the ends of the V lines with their many noise makers. The Rajah arrived. I watched him carefully as he checked out the set-up, being especially careful of the 'no noise' rule. "All right," he said in a loud whisper, "Ted and June take your places on the machan. Then Mrs. Flaiz, you climb up and sit next to them. Pastor Flaiz and I will take this lower machan." With that he handed Mom a gun and helped her up the tree. I couldn't have been more excited had I been on my way to the moon! Me in a tree with the Rajah waiting to get a tiger! It doesn't get bigger than that!

Breathlessly I watched the Rajah. He fished for something in a pocket. Taking it out I saw that it was a little hand pistol. He reached in again and brought out a bullet. Placing it in its pocket, he looked around, lifted his arm, and pulled the trigger. The jungle exploded. Unbelievable.

Yelling, banging, whistling, car horns. You name it—it was there. The plan was that if a tiger showed up first my Dad would shoot it. If a leopard or hyena came by my Mom would get it with her lesser gun. (The Rajah didn't want my Mom to be shooting a gun with such a powerful kick back as the ones Dad and he were using. He was there just for back up if needed.)

A wild boar with three little piglets came dashing out from some bushes nearby. The Rajah indicated with his hand not to bother. We watched for any sign of stripes in the bushes. Any movement? I saw a jackal slip out at one

The Rajah's Trophy

point, but it raised no interest. The noise was coming closer and closer. No self respecting tiger would put up with all that noise. He would be gone in a minute. Still we kept on watching, hoping against hope that one or two of them would still bound out of the jungle thickets. But no. They weren't there.

It was disappointing, but we had gone through the hunt and seen how it worked. The Rajah had brought out a surprise for everyone, hundreds of coconuts for the crowd. With a machete the men cut off the heads and passed them around and every one drank to the full. By telling stories of other hunts taken with the Rajah, it was a splendid afternoon.

~ thirty-nine ~

Ted and the Leopard Attack

Quickly Dad turned around to check on his big gun.

One morning, bright and early, Ted and Dad took off for Suthikinda. This was a nearby village where a man lived who was good with the placing of tile. There was a new area in the hospital that needed a flooring of tile, and Dad wanted to be sure that he got the very best. We told them good-bye. Shortly Punkie came over to play in the tree house with Ketchup and me. The day flew by and that evening she asked me to have supper with them. I called to Mother and that was fine with her. Punkie had two big balls that we could just barely get our arms around. They were such fun to play with so following supper she got them out, and we were having a great time. Shortly Mrs. Coyne announced that it was seven thirty–time for bed.

"I'll walk home with you, then you walk half way home with me," said Punkie. That was the usual way we parted.

"There's a bright moon out tonight so we don't have to carry a lantern," I added. "Why don't we bounce the balls both ways?"

Before starting I glanced up to notice that our front veranda was lighted by two lanterns, but I saw no details. We bounced our way to our house singing as we went. When we reached the bottom of the stairs I looked up and froze.

"Oh no!" I screamed. "No. No." For there, on the veranda, was a big leopard crouched and ready to pounce on Punkie and me. Screaming and running at full pace we cleared the half way spot between the two houses. Just about then we heard Ted yell. I turned to look and see if the leopard had gotten Ted. We saw that the leopard was still in the same position with Ted sitting beside him. "What's he doing?" I asked in amazement.

When we saw how casually Ted was petting the leopard we cautiously returned to the house. "He's a nice leopard. He won't hurt you," Ted chuckled.

It was then that the truth came out. As Dad and Ted made their way home, two leopards crossed the path in front of them. Dad remembered just then that the tile man had told him of a leopard that had killed a buffalo near their village—just two days before. Quickly Dad turned around to check on his big gun. Was it in the car? It was! Knowing the price that the farmers have to pay for having a leopard around that kills their livestock, Dad felt duty bound to take them out.

He stopped the car and turned on his powerful spot light. One of the leopards stopped, turned around, and crouching down seemed unable to figure out just what was going on. The other one slipped through the trees into the jungle and out of sight. Dad grabbed the gun from the back seat hoping not to frighten the leopard. He was able to catch him in the crosshairs and pull the trigger. It was a clear hit and after a few minutes with the spot light directly on the leopard, it became evident that he was truly finished.

At that point, they loaded the leopard onto the car, and when they reached home, Ted got the servants to help him position the leopard on the veranda in the scariest possible position. "This will really take care of Junie and Punkie," he said to the servants rubbing his hands with glee. And it did!

***

Every year each mission family can pick and choose just where they want to go for the next year's family vacation. This particular summer we had chosen to go to Darjeeling high in the Himalayas of eastern India. It was a resort area deluged in the summer time by the elite of the sub continent—the English, the wealthy of India, the diplomatic chore, etc. My favorite memory of Darjeeling was the huge expansive view looking northward of the third highest mountain in the world—Kanchenjunga. In the morning sun it looked so majestic, so powerful with its enormous ice fields being broken here and there by jagged cliffs and precipitous outcroppings.

Dad caught the cattle killer

Dad explained to Ted and me that just before we were to leave Darjeeling we were going to take a hike to Tiger Mountain. We were going to get up at two o'clock, get on a horse, and ride for three hours up to the top of the mountain. Why? Why were we going to do this? Because from that spot—on a clear day—you can see Mt. Everest—the highest mountain in the world.

Well, that sounded pretty exciting to us. And my folks had no trouble in waking us up that morning. We rode out

Dad and the end of a cattle killer

of town and joined a group of about thirty others—all on horses. Our interest, of course, was on the weather. Would clouds be covering the summit of Everest? Just as we were nearing the top of Tiger Mountain we could detect a change in the color of the sky. It was getting light! As the sun was coming up our guide was explaining just which peak was Everest. What a sight it was—not a cloud in the sky!

We stayed there for about an hour before starting back. Many of the folks wanted to take pictures and just enjoy the sight of the mountain. When we got back to our cabin I noticed little black things all over my legs and arms. When I went to pull one off, it stretched out to about four inches and snapped back.

“Hey, what are these little black things?” asked Ted, pulling on one from his leg.

“I’ve got some too,” added Mom. “They just don’t let go.” We all waited for Dad to come to the rescue. He was heading for some tweezers in the bathroom cupboard and with them he was able to squeeze the head and pull them out. We realized that we had come to an area where these worms lived, and while going through the forest on the horses, they had grabbed onto us from the leaves of the trees.

~ forty ~

Big Trouble

The policemen tell me that the penalty for such is jail....

There is a place in India called Kodi. A more beautiful place cannot be imagined. Huge tropical trees, many of them dressed and decorated with large flowers, exquisitely etched in the colors that only the tropics can create. Beautiful vines hanging down from high branches where monkeys swing and sway. Highly colored birds fly into the picture to add sparkle to the background. Wild elephants add their part by trumpeting and giving to the jungle that magical feel.

As summer drew near, we were faced with the decision of where we would go for our summer holiday.

"How about Missouri—so you can go to school," Mom suggested.

An emphatic "No," from Ted and me. "Let's go to Kodi," I said. "Punkie and Freddie are going there, and we've only been there once before. It would be so much fun to go with them." And so it was. (Mom was a very giving person.)

Kodi was also a resort area for the rich of India. Its beauty was unmatched anywhere. Up on the side of a hill were five little bungalows where we had stayed before. At the foot of the hill was a rather nice home where the owner of the cottages lived—a Mrs. Grimes. One of the houses was taken by the Coyne's - Punkie's family. We would be taking one, and the other three were to be occupied by missionaries from other parts of India.

"They're here! They're here!" Punkie was yelling from behind our two cabins. I laid down the suitcase that I had been lugging from the bus station and dashed outside to see if it could be true. It was! The little crab family that we had been playing with so long ago was still in the creek. (We didn't stop to wonder if these just might be the great-great-grand kids of the originals), but instead ran around the hill checking out to see if all was as it should be with no changes.

"Hey, Junie, my bedroom window is just across from yours. See?" Sure enough. We could talk together–just like at home. The afternoon went fast–opening up suitcases–deciding which cupboards to put what in. Ted and I would occupy the bedroom next to the Coyne's bungalow, and Dad and Mom would take the larger one with the beautiful view of the rain forest to the west of them.

It was now evening–the settling in had been done, and it was time to say goodnight to Punkie. I called from my window. "Hey, Punkie, tomorrow I'll show you the jungle where we found the baby deer."

"And don't forget the eagle's nest."

"O.K., if it's still there."

"Nite."

"G'Nite."

It was a beautiful day-not a cloud in the sky. I was anxious to get outside to check on the crab family. How they managed to get along without my directions for all of this time was a miracle to me. I took along some crumbs to feed them with. I also took the smooth stones that I found in the stream and built some little homes for them to live in. Punkie soon joined me and together we had a great time building mansions for these tiny crabs.

"You guys want to have some fun?" Ted had just come out to see what we were doing. "What's up?" I asked.

"Well, you know that Mrs. Grimes has a tin roof. So Freddie and I thought it would be fun to drop some little stones onto it and let them roll off. She is such an old grouch–she deserves it. Mom and Dad went to town and won't know anything about it." Just then Freddie arrived and off they went to carry out their cherished plan. "Let's go and see what happens," I said.

The cabins that we had rented stood on the hillside and were reached by a switch back path with Mrs. Grimes being at the bottom of the hill. There were some trees lining the pathway and to the left of her home was a big pile of huge boulders. What fun it was running over them! The boys picked up a few tiny pebbles and tossed them onto her roof. Nothing happened–like somebody coming out and yelling at us. Then they picked up a few more but this time they were a little bigger. We watched them roll down the corrugated tin roof –bump, bump, bang, bang, but again–nothing happened. I'm not sure just what it was that we were hoping to see–Mrs. Grimes coming out to find us? Or maybe a servant doing the same? We were well hidden behind a tree or a boulder but as time passed we became braver, and the rocks became bigger. After one throw the back door opened and out came Singh, her servant, with a curse. He looked for us but couldn't find us.

We had an advantage—the gift of time. Singh browsed around, for a while, kicked a few boulders, cursed again, and finally disappeared into the house. It was some time later that we had the courage to try again, perhaps fifteen to twenty minutes.

"Shall we try again?" asked Ted in a loud whisper.

"Yeah, let's do," I said emphatically. "Mrs. Grimes is always so cross. Maybe this will help her to be sweet and kind." Slowly we crept out of our hiding place, got some big rocks—about the size of an apple, and threw them on the roof. Singh was waiting. Waiting just behind the door! Out he came with a roar, "I'm going to get you guys and see that the police put you in jail." (He, of course, was talking in Telegue.) Then he started chasing us. Around and around we went. Because of his sandals and their slippery souls he couldn't maneuver the huge boulders. We kids were bare footed and our feet clung to the stone. Pretty soon one of the boys started teasing him. "What's the matter, Singh? You getting tired?" This made him furious. Again he tried to conquer the boulders, but all he could do was slip and slide.

This continued on for quite some time. We kids would almost let him catch us then sprint on ahead and out of reach—letting him stew in his own resentment. With a "You'll be sorry. Just you wait and see," and with his fist shaking above his head, he disappeared into the house.

It was the next day, a beautiful day full of promise. Punkie and I were skip roping up and down the switch back path. The sun was not too hot—but then it wasn't too cool either—actually just right. The birds were singing up a storm as our friend, a bunny rabbit, was browsing in the grass next to the stream. "What a pretty day," I said to Punkie. Just too pretty to let it pass without comment, I decided.

"Where are you going, Dad—so early in the morning?" Dad was stepping out of the front door and hurrying down the path toward the village. "Just a little business - some exercise," he said with a smile and a wave. "I'll see you before long."

Punkie and I spent the rest of the day playing with the crab family and introducing them to different foods. We noted that their favorite was a tiny piece of boiled egg—left over from breakfast. Second in line was bread crumbs. Oh, how they did love bread crumbs. They would fight over them like you wouldn't believe. I decided that Ketchup was missing out on some fun times so went inside to get her. Finding a small bush near the crabs I put down a little blanket and settled her so that she could "see" them fighting. Some of their mansions were in need of restoration so Punkie and I set about to fix that problem.

Early afternoon, Dad returned and with him some mangos and bananas. Along about four o'clock we looked up to see two policemen starting up the path to our house. Because of their outstanding dress code, when seeing a policeman one is struck with fear and admiration at the same time. Fear—should there be any irregularity in one's public behavior of late. Admiration—the yellow uniform is just so glamorous that it's hard to not be affected by it.

But why? Why would the police be coming toward our house we wondered? Maybe they will break away and go in another direction. But no—they just kept on coming. And the closer they came to us the more frightened we became. "They look so nice," said Punkie. "Look. They're smiling—so they can't be too bad." One of them pulled out his police club and swung it around in a fancy design, but still they kept on coming. Pretty soon they would be to a spot where our house would be the only one left. And sure enough as they neared the spot they turned to the left and started up our walk.

"Let's hide," whispered Punkie. She grabbed my hand and together we crept in the back door and headed for the bedroom closet. My heart was racing full speed. Yesterday? Why was yesterday so big to me now? Suddenly we saw Ted and Freddie tip-toeing up to the door. Seeing them reminded us of our experience the day before. Could it be? Could it really be that the police had heard about it? All about our throwing rocks on Mrs. Grime's house?

"Good afternoon, Sahib," said the lead police man, "a beautiful afternoon."

"Yes indeed," answered Dad. "Here. Have a seat." Dad was on the porch and carefully he helped the two men to chairs. "Tell me," he said "How can I help you gentleman?"

"We understand that you have two boys living here with you," answered the policeman.

"We do," said Dad. "Two fine young men. One is our son. The other is a friend's son."

"And is it true that you also have two girls living with you?" This was just too much. How, I wondered, does one live through these experiences? My heart was beating to a crescendo. Punkie, I could see, was going through the same frightening situation as I. Through my tears I peeked out of the crack in the door–to see how the boys were doing, but they were hiding behind the heavy curtains in the front room and only the bottom of their pants could be seen.

"Yes," said Dad, "We also have two girls. One is our daughter. The other is a friend's daughter."

"Well, we have come to get all four of them–we'll be taking them to jail."

"Jail?" asked Dad incredulous. "Why jail?"

"For throwing stones on Mrs. Grime's roof."

"They would do that?" repeated Dad. "Throw stones on Mrs. Grime's roof? It's hard to believe, but I suppose that you are telling the truth so we have to take your word seriously." With that Dad got up from his chair, cupped his hands to his mouth and called loudly," Ted and Freddie, come here. I need you."

I thought that my life had come to a standstill. Punkie was whispering, "What'll we doooooooo? Oh, what will we do when our folks go back to America? They'll have to leave us."

"And Tommy Tucker," I wailed. "What will happen to him? Can I take Ketchup to jail with me? It's all just too terrible...too terrible to even think about."

There was Ted and Freddie crawling out from behind the curtains. I looked closely and saw that their faces were wet with tears. "Boys, I would like for you to meet two Kodi policemen," said Dad. 'They have come to take you to jail." A silence followed. No one spoke. Then–

"We didn't m...e...a........... " Freddie was trying to speak. Ted then tried, "You see ...we...were....j...u...s...." when he broke down and cried some more.

"Did you or did you not throw some rocks on Mrs. Grime's roof?" asked Dad.

"Well, yes, but you see we were just trying to have some fun." By this time Freddie had overcome his fear of talking and was trying to put up something of a defense. "How about you, Ted, didn't you think that this was fun?"

"Yes," he stammered.

"June and Punkie, wherever you are, I need you," Dad called. Slowly we crept out of the closet and onto the front porch. Dad was saying to us girls, "I have been talking to the boys and they tell me that throwing stones was fun. Was that your idea too?"

"Yeah," we both answered.

"O.K. guys. The policemen tell me that the penalty for such is jail. They want you to get your pajamas, toothbrush, and other necessities, and they will take you there. It was nice of them to come and get you."

"Hurry up and we will be on our way." The in-charge policeman was talking and getting up from his chair at the same time.

"It was fun," said Freddie, " but now we know that we shouldn't have done it."

"I'm sorry, too," said Ted.

"How about you girls?" asked Dad.

"Me too. Me too," we answered in unison. "We're all sorry."

"Tell me, Sir," Dad said as he spoke directly to the policeman, "If a person is genuinely sorry for what he has done, does that help him to be excused of the penalty?"

"It can," he answered. "I would like to talk to all four of you kids. Come here and stand in front of me for a minute." We all scrambled to be first in line, anything to please the policeman. "Are you truly sorry for what you did? And will you be tempted to do it again?" We all answered together with, "We promise. We promise we'll never do it again. Yes, we're so sorry that we did it. No, we'll never ever—EVER—do it again."

"Well," said the policeman," they sound pretty convincing. Tell you what we'll do. I have your promise that it will never happen again. So on that promise we will let you off this time. But should it ever happen again you know the penalty."

Shaking hands with the head policeman, Dad in a very low monotone said, "Thanks for your help, Sir." This was followed by a wink and with that they were off spinning their clubs as they descended the downward trail.

Policemen, we decided, were very nice men.

~ forty-one ~

The Revenge

"I know that when people get mad about something - they sue."

The lazy days of summer progressed through the month of July. Hiking the beautiful hills of Kodi, stirring up the elk in the gullies, teasing the monkeys as they clamored for attention, and boating on the peaceful lake all comprised the various activities of the day.

"Who wants to go for a hike to Drop Off Mountain?" asked Mom early one morning. "Let's see. It will be happening on Tuesday–day after tomorrow. Everyone's going. We're told to bring our lunch 'cause it will take six hours–round trip."

"I can't tell you my answer until I talk to Punkie," I informed Mom. Ted was gung-ho over the plan, as I knew he would be. Punkie came over shortly and together we discussed the plan. It would be fun we decided to just stay home and relax. Relax and play with the crabs. We would be leaving Kodi in a few days, and the crabs needed their homes rebuilt and secured. Yeah. That's what we needed to do.

Mom wasn't too happy over the idea and neither was Mrs. Coyne, but they decided that we were old enough to be left alone for that length of time. When Tuesday arrived we hugged and kissed them all good-bye. Mom had given us plenty of advice–advice that could last for years. We were sure of that.

What a day! All the crowd had gone and it was quiet. Punkie and I felt like the Kings of a castle. Nobody was there to tell us what we could and couldn't do. We could eat anything and everything we wanted, play any game we wanted, or read any book we wanted. What joy! What total joy!

Along about two o'clock we decided to go indoors at Punkie's house to get a snack. We heard Mrs. Grimes call her servant, "Singh, Singh, I need you," her voice started us to thinking. "You know, Punkie, I don't think Mrs. G. has ever had to feel bad about what she did to us."

"And that's kinda too bad," agreed Punkie, "Everyone needs to feel a little bad when they have hurt someone." The girls pondered over Punkie's statement–it was just the psyc....psyc....hol... .Oh, you know what I mean. The ...... psych....olo...ology of it all. Anyone could see that.

"Agreed," I announced. A long silence followed. "Do you think that.......that....."

"Singh. Singh," Mrs. G. was calling again and that gave me more courage. "You know what, Punkie. I'll bet there are plenty more rocks there above Mrs. G's place. What do you think?"

"Oh, no," said Punkie. "No. No. You remember what we promised the policemen. If there are any more rocks, we go to jail."

"Yeah, that's true but what can we do to make her feel bad about?" We cast our eyes about the place and noticed the lovely furniture. The sofa was a rust colored piece of work–beautiful to look at with a big tapestry filling the center back. We looked at the bedroom. It had one large bed with twin beds to the side, all of them with matching bedspreads. Mrs. G did have good taste, we decided.

"What do you say, Punkie, we do something to the bedroom? If we want her to really feel bad we can cut up the mattresses. That would make her apologize to us for what she did."

"Yeah," said Punkie. "That's a good idea. We have a couple of pairs of big scissors we can use." As she hunted for the scissors I pulled off the bedspreads and sheets. This was getting exciting. "I wonder if Mrs. G. will come up to our homes to apologize."

"Maybe she'll just write us a note."

"Yeah, I think I'd like that better," I said.

Punkie got on one side and I on the other. We started cutting on the big bed first. We found that the mattress was stuffed with cotton. Without the cloth to hold it down the cotton started floating around the room. And soon, very soon, we were sneezing up a storm.

"How should we cut up this mattress?" I asked Punkie. "Into small bits or big pieces?"

"Well, I think about a foot big would do a good job," she answered holding up a piece of mattress covering about that size.

"Looks good to me," I said.

Things settled down to a quiet hum. Both of us were thrilled with the apology we were to hear possibly that very night. "I wonder what our folks will say to Mrs. G.," I ventured. "Maybe they will tell her that they are going to sue her. Is this a good thing to sue about?" I wondered.

"Don't know," said Punkie, "but I think it could be. I know that when people get mad about something they sue. And we're sure mad about what she did."

"Yeah."

The big bed took a long time. When finished we started on the single beds—Punkie taking one and me the other.

"Let's make it really look good," I said. "Pull out the cotton and spread it all around." This part was fun. By the handfuls we pulled it out and strew it over the house. Living room. Kitchen. And of course the bedroom. We threw the pieces of cut cloth around the bedroom and took notice that the house was hazy with cotton.

"Let's go to my house and wait for the folks to come home. What a surprise it will be for them. They're going to love it." As we walked through the living room I glanced back and my eye caught a glimpse of the beautiful sofa. That tapestry back there was just too pretty to ignore. "Ketchup would love to have a dress made from it," I explained. Quickly, I cut it out, and we were on our way.

"Oh, there's Mrs. G. working in her garden," said Punkie, looking down to the bottom of the hill. Her corn and tomatoes were unbeatable and many were the times that Punkie and I wished that we could just help ourselves to some.

"I don't feel very good," said Punkie. "I wonder when all the crowd will be home."

"Don't know but come to think about it, I don't feel very good either." We started looking for a game to play but soon lost interest. A book to read? Lost interest there too.

Soon we just sat down on the back porch and looked into space.

"Why don't you feel good?" I asked Punkie.

"Dunno." A long pause followed. Then, "I was just wondering where my mom and dad are going to sleep tonight. That goes for Freddie and me too."

"Oh my goodness. I never thought about that," I said. "Did you think about it?"

"No," said Punkie with the tears starting to run down her cheeks. "All I thought about was how sorry Mrs. G. would be for having hurt us."

"Me too," I said. Then I felt them—the tears streaming down my own face. We sat for sometime in silence struggling with the problem. The crowd would be home soon, and we would have to come up with an answer.

"It's oh so awful to even think about. What'll we do, Punkie, run away and hide?"

"There's no place that we can hide," she answered.

Soon we heard the cheery sounds of the crowd returning. "I'm going to hide in your closet," said Punkie, forgetting her words of a few minutes ago. Quickly we barged into the closet and closed the door tightly.

"Wonder where the girls are." That was Dr. Coyne talking just behind the house. "Punkie. Junie. Where are you?" I was afraid my heart would stop. What could we tell them? How could we soften the blow? It was all so—just out there.

"Junie, where are you?" That was Mom, but there was no way that I could go out and face her. The crowd chatted some more before going to their individual homes.

"Oh my goodness," Mrs. Coyne blurted out as she opened her door. We could hear her from the closet in our house. Then with a higher decibel level, "Who...Who...Who could have done this?" I grabbed Punkie's hand and held on tight, hoping somehow that it could get me through.

"We have to find the girls. They would know who did it." This statement reminded me of the two or three people we had heard that morning saying, "The girls are such responsible kids, I'm sure that they will be fine being left alone." Remembering that hurt now. With many more calls, Mom became suspicious of that closed closet door. She hadn't seen what we had done but listening to Mrs. Coyne she knew that it was pretty bad. Punkie and I had choked up our crying, but when Mom opened the door we couldn't hold it back any more. What a sight she beheld, two crying girls' voices blending into a high wail.

"I'm sooooo sorry, Mom," is as far as I got.

"Me too," added Punkie. More wailing.

"We did it all," said Punkie. "We just thought that Mrs. Grimes was feeling bad because of hurting us kids." Time out for more crying. Then, "So you see we were giving her a chance to apologize to us."

"I'm having a little trouble following your train of logic," said Mom.

"But I guess we better go over now and see what can be done about it."

We made a sorry sight trudging over to the Coyne's house. Mrs. Grimes was still in her garden. "Best to ya," she called with a wave of her hand. Oh my goodness! In just one moment they're going to see it all.

It was then that I heard Mom's gasp, but to hear Dad's was just more than I could take. Escape! Escape! Anywhere? But where could I go? I had to get out. Let me out of here. I turned to run—to run as fast as I could go—but just then I felt a firm hand on my shoulder.

"Listen here, Punkin, there'll be no running away from this. You'll see it through with us." When Dad talked like that I knew that it was final—there was no appeal.

Punkie and I chose to sit in a corner of the living room while the parents checked out the destruction. We couldn't hear their plotting and decision making, but we could see their shock of noticing various disturbances of the place. Finally they sat down and came to a decision on what to do.

They sat at the table and had us stand in front of them. Dad talked and told us the significance of what we had done. It was criminal he said and if the policemen heard of it they would want to put us in prison. We were in India to make Christians of the people, and this was certainly not the way to do it. O.K. By way of punishment he explained that there was nothing that would match or be equal for punishment against what we had done. But the best that they could come up with was an apology to Mrs. Grimes and a giving of our monthly allowance to some poor little Indian for a year.

The giving of our allowance was nothing. It was the apology to Mrs. Grimes that was overwhelming. "O.K., we'll do it before we leave for home. Some time," I answered stoically.

"You will do it right now, Miss Junie. Right now! Did you hear me?"

Dr. Coyne took a hold of Punkie's hand, and Dad took a hold of mine. Our mothers followed just behind as we started down the hill.

What added to the indignity of it all was the sudden appearance of Ted and Freddie. Around the side of the house they came whistling, laughing, and shooting stones with their sling shots.

Punkie and Junie

"What's going on?" they asked in unison—their faces—one big question mark. "My goodness. What did happen?"

"We'll answer that question when we get back," said Dad. We continued on down the hill deep into our own thoughts. What on earth will Mrs. G. say? What will she do?

"Good afternoon, Mrs. Grimes," said Dad with a nod of his head. She stood, shaking off the dirt from her apron.

"What brings you folks out on this beautiful afternoon?" she asked pleasantly.

"Well, I have two little girls who have something they want to say to you." Silence reigned for some time. Just being near Mrs. Grimes was overwhelming enough but to have to talk to her was more than I could bear. The tears started flowing. I glanced at Punkie. She was in the same situation. Except for the sound of sobbing, there was nothing but silence.

"Girls, we're waiting," said Dad.

"I can't...I just can't," I stumbled out. Punkie could do no better. Finally Dad stepped in with, "I'm sorry, Mrs. Grimes, but it seems that the girls are speechless. Perhaps if I make the confession, we can let Punkie and June agree. How's that?" By now Mrs. Grimes seemed clueless. She would look at Punkie first then at me hoping for a word of explanation, but there was nothing.

"I'll go up," she said taking off her apron. "I want to see what they have done."

"That won't be necessary, Mrs. Grimes. We will have everything in order before you know it. But first I must tell you that the girls disrupted some things in the Coyne's house, and I am sure that they are sorry for it now. Am I right, girls?" We nodded our heads but Dad wasn't impressed.

"Punkie and June, your parents have come down here to Mrs. Grime's house with you to help rectify the awful situation you left us in the house. I've spoken of it to Mrs. Grimes, and it seems to me that the very least you girls could do is to tell her that you are sorry."

My Dad is the most patient, kind, and peaceful person that one could find anywhere, but when I see such a determined expression on his face I know that it is time for me to give up. "I'm....I'm.....well, I mean....I'm just so, so sorry, Mrs. Grimes," followed by a flood of tears.

"How about you, Punkie?" asked Dr. Coyne. Punkie came through with the same. Some niceties closed the conversation, and we were on our way hone.

We found out the next day that there was in town a store owned by some British people. Fortunately they had in their inventory some household items which we were in dire need of–many double mattresses but only one small one. The store man offered to cut down one of the large size mattresses to fit the small bed which made our moms delighted. A sofa very similar to the destroyed one was also available.

That night at worship time my Dad expressed in a most delighted manner the appreciation he felt toward God for having solved our great difficulties. He chose as the worship verse that evening, "All things work together for good to them that love God." And when Mrs. Grimes was invited to come and take a look, her comment was, "What did the girls do to the place? I can't see any difference." Punkie and I learned a good lesson from that hard, hard experience.

~ forty-two ~

The Magic Show

"You gonna tell Mom and Dad?" asked Ted.

"I'm not. How about you?" I replied.

"Not me..."

Finally the day came—the day I had to say good-bye to Punkie. How I wondered—could I ever continue with life with no Punkie to share the fun, the scary experiences, the elephant rides, the swimming pool games, and the bicycle rides? Then there was shouting "Good night" to each other across the abyss. She had no sister. Nor did I. No. We filled that gap for each other and now we were parting. We would see each other again in America some time, but it would never be the same, for when I got there Punkie would be all grown up and sophisticated, and I would still be the jungle walla of long ago.

We made promises to each other—promises that we would never change—promises that we would meet again sometime in India as grown up missionaries. We would keep Lilly and Ketchup with us until that end, and things could carry on as now. But nothing. Absolutely nothing—not all the imaginings nor prophecies prepared me for that day—the day that I had to actually say good-bye to my Punkie.

***

One afternoon I was sitting on the veranda at home playing with Tommy Tucker. He along with two of his best friends were scampering around trying to get the nuts that I was tossing to them. Though I could tell the difference between Tommy and his friends—he being much larger—he was always so cuddly with me. His friends this day would keep a respectful distance from me; probably about a six foot unseen circle enclosed me from them. Tom, however, would sit on my lap and flip his tail. A slow flipping meant contentment. A rapid flipping with a chirping sound meant excitement. Today he was excited–jumping on my lap–climbing to my shoulder then back again to my lap, watching carefully as I tossed a piece of cashew nut to them. He was trying to beat them in getting to the punch line first. In fact there was so much excitement going on that I failed to notice two Indian men coming up behind us.

"What can I do for you?" I asked a little surprised by their sudden appearance.

"We do magic, and we were wondering if we could show you some of it." I thought for a moment. Mom and Dad had discouraged Ted and me from people like this to perform for us. The devil, they say, takes advantage of some folks and if accepted into a group he feels that he can stay and do all of the harm he wants to. True. But they were already here, and it's kinda fun just seeing what they can do. "So sure. Go ahead." At that point Ted came around the corner wondering what was going on. I explained to him, and he was all right with it.

One of the men fished into his bag and pulled out a carved dog, maybe six inches long. He walked to the end of the veranda, pulled over a chair, climbed it, and carefully inspected the rafter. He then motioned us to come to him.

"You see I am putting this dog up on the rafter. I want both of you to take a look at the rafter and see if the dog is all that's there." We both got on the chair and strained to see the up side of the rafter, but we weren't tall enough.

Some of Dad's books in the next room took care of the situation.

"You're right. Nothing else is up there," said Ted.

"Now we will go back to the other side of the veranda," said the man. When we got there he knelt down on the veranda, put his hands under his shirt, and started saying a whole lot of hocus pocus things. (He, of course, was talking in Telegue as they knew no English.)

Finally he said, "It's time to go back." So back we went and climbed the chair. No dog. Turned around and here he was with the dog in his hands.

"You gotta do that again," I said. "I didn't watch you carefully enough."

I took the dog from his hands, climbed the chair, and placed the dog on the rafter then got down, and we all walked to the starting place. I kept the man right beside me all the time. He proceeded to put his hands in his shirt again, knelt down on the veranda, and started with his hocus pocus rendition coming to the end in about three minutes. Again we all went to see if the dog was there. Again - no dog, but there it was in the man's hands. We insisted that they do it a number of times which they did willingly. Ted got to thinking that this was something that they simply could not do on their own—that Dad and Mom's judgment on the subject was no doubt right. He went to his dresser, got a few annas to give to the men, and they felt well paid.

"You gonna tell Mom and Dad?" asked Ted.

"I'm not. How about you?"

"Not me." Ted thought for awhile as he watched the two men disappear behind the back hedge. "Wasn't that something?" Ted looked incredulous. "I'd say that the old devil is a pretty sharp guy. But you know what? I don't think that I will hang around him again anytime soon."

~ forty-three ~

The Broken Record

"Your face is a giveaway. You never have been able to tell me a lie and get away with it."

In my folk's bedroom -downstairs- sat our family victrola. How we loved to listen to it play the pretty songs of long ago. It seemed a frivolous thing to bring clear across the ocean, but so often one of the family would comment on the fun of having it with us and that would settle the question. We would wake up in the morning with the swing of a song playing downstairs. I knew that Mom and Dad would be down there in front of the victrola doing their exercises in sync to that happy tune. Before leaving America, Mom had the fun of choosing a big supply of records. She picked old favorites–*My Wild Irish Rose*, *My Old Kentucky Home*, *Sewanee River*, etc. One of my favorites of the group was a lively jive song called *I'm Happy in My Blue Heaven*. And when the choice was ours, that was pretty much always Ted's and mine.

One night I remember sitting in the dining room playing with the frogs under the table. Mom and Dad were reading a news magazine from America which had just arrived and which was always a big event. Dad was going through an article, reading aloud regarding the state of jazz in America. Played by the big swing bands of the period, it was sweeping the country. Toward the end of the article the author brought up the worry that the churches of the nation had concerning the jazz phenomena. What is happening to the country? Where is it going to end?

Mom and Dad's account didn't pass me by. I had seen on the record a note that this rendition was a new one for the song. Thump! Thump! Thump! Just to think that there was a horrible, sinful record polluting our home. Mom probably wasn't even aware that this was a jazz production. I'll have to get rid of it some way—but how?

The next day it was first on my line-up. Being such a tremendous record it needed a stunning closer to match. Again I needed the men servants to observe my authority. Except for Mosha, they were all four of them grown men. Had I been older and able to understand their facial expressions correctly I'm sure that I would have been mightily embarrassed.

They were called and stood on the veranda, chairless. I had the record. Holding it up above my head with both hands I explained what I was doing. This record was such an evil thing, I said, that it needed to be broken. My mother hadn't been aware of its nature so when I explain it to her she will be so glad that I have taken care of it. Then in a most dramatic way I brought down the record, smashing it against the veranda rock into a thousand pieces. I dismissed the servants, got a broom, and cleaned up the pieces.

It must have been two or three weeks before the record was found missing. Mom had chosen it for exercises that morning, but where—oh where, could it be?

"June, have you seen the record, *My Blue Heaven*, anywhere? I can't find it."

I knew that this moment would come, but I wasn't ready for it. Do I put her off or do I face it right now? That was the big question. "Well, I don't know, Mom. I wonder if maybe you left it in the office some time."

"No, I've looked there."

"I heard you and Mrs. Coyne talking about that record one time. I'll bet you loaned it to her."

"No, I've never loaned out any of those records." Mom put her hands on her hips and looked me through and through. "Look here, little Miss, you have a pretty hard time faking me out. Your face is a giveaway. You never have been able to tell me a lie and get away with it."

By now I was tearing up and ducking my head. "What did you do with it, Honey?

"Well, ...I.....I... thought that....," and the story all came tumbling out with sobs and tears.

"I do appreciate your looking out for Dad and me, Honey, but I would have appreciated you talking it over with me first. I had never thought of that record as being jazz. I just thought of it as being a fun piece and a good one for exercising with. So cheer up, Sweetie, and just remember next time to come and talk to me first." She said this last with a tweak of my chin and the bringing out of a reluctant smile. Mom had a way with her—a way that nobody else could match.

~ forty-four ~

Good-bye... Again

"How could I possibly give up and trade all of this beauty for the likes of America?"

And now....well....and now it is time to say good-bye to India, the India that I loved. This was the India that held all of the beautiful Himalayan Mountains in her northern tier, the first of the Seven Wonders of the World–the Taj Mahal, the fabulous jungles that gave room to the tigers, the leopards of the world. And not to mention the herds of buffaloes and the slow plodding camels winding their way through the huts and villages of India. How could I possibly give up and trade all of this beauty for the likes of America?

I had heard of the mountains of America, beautiful and serene, but where their heights? I had also heard of their buildings–their polish and their fashion–such as the Washington monument, but where the intricate beauty of the Taj? And, yes, your sandy white beaches. They're beautiful but where the palm strewn warmth of the Indian shore line?

Punkie and Freddie had left India a few months before and ...well this was it! This was the day that I had been dreading for such a long, long time. When I said good bye to Punkie it was as if something had died within me, something of the beauty of India had just vanished. Mom, in her encouraging way, said that the beauty would come back–just hold on and I would see. And sure enough she was right.

Our family was standing on the front veranda of our home; Dad and Mom were telling the multitude of people good-bye. In the preceding days we had gone through the various farewells that such an occasion seems to precipitate. I was holding Ketchup, and Tommy was on my shoulder flipping his tail. For some time I seemed oblivious to what was going on around me as I talked to Tommy.

"Tommy. Tommy Tucker. How can I leave you, Tommy? How can I say good-bye? You know that I have been trying my very, very best—and Dad and Mom too—to get you on the ship with us. But the answer was always, "No." So next best we asked Mosha, who loves you as we do, to be your parent, to keep you just as we have. He was thrilled with this responsibility. "

Gently I took him down, hugged and petted him. "Just one more time, Tommy. I have to see you in the light of the tree house where we have spent so many happy hours reading, studying and sleeping." I ran with him to the mango tree which housed our tree house, climbed the ladder, and with tears streaming down my cheeks, I laid him on the floor and gently stroked his back. In a moment he turned over thereby asking me to rub his tummy.

"When I come back to India, Mosha told me that he would give you back to me, and we could have fun together again. Don't feel bad, Tommy, 'cause I'll bring Ketchup with me and we'll have the playhouse to play in again. Be careful of those civet cats though, Tommy, and don't let them get you."

By now they were calling from the house. "Junie! Junie! Where are you? We've got to go."

I handed Tommy to Mosha and hopped in the car. I couldn't see for crying. Slowly the car moved out of the parking space. I opened my eyes one more time to see so many people crying and calling out endearing terms. But a flash of Tom was worth it all. He was sitting atop Mosha's shoulder flipping his tail and chatting up a storm. It saved for me that one last picture that I would always treasure.

Sitting on the front steps of our house

~ forty-five ~

America, But Not Forever

"...you know how big white people have always scared me." And I was sure that I would always be afraid of them here.

"O....I....N....K. Oink. "What is that oink business anyway, Mom?" I sat up in my cot and looked around. "Oh my goodness! Where are we?" Slowly the scenes of the night before started materializing in my mind.

We had left the ship—The Europa—four days before, bought a car (a Chevy—not new but almost), and had traversed a number of miles already. "The last state line that we had crossed was—now let me see—was it Ohio? No. No. In...d...ia. That was it. India. But it had something else stuck on the end of it." "Ana," said Mom, "Indiana." I remember when I heard the name for the first time thinking that it must be a beautiful state with a name so close to India.

We had traveled all day. Now it was late at night, and I was getting sleepy. I looked over to see what Ted was up to and saw that he was sound asleep.

"We need to find a place to spend the night," said Dad. He was bent forward and staring out at the passing terrain. This was before the days of many motels so people either slept in their cars or just spread out a little pup tent with army cots.

"There's the place. Look, Ted. Right over there to the left." It was Mom grabbing Dad's arm and pointing to a spot on his side of the car. It was a pretty little valley that came together in a stream. The moon was almost full and gave considerable help in setting up camp. One, two, three, four Army cots. Dad had them up in no time. He lined them up on the side of the car—opposite the highway. That was the last that I remembered ...until now.

"Oh. Oh. That OINK belongs to the big pig. The one I see poking around in the mud by the creek. Hey, more pigs—little ones too." Now with my eyes wide open I followed the driveway up, up to the top of the hill where a little white house stood, surrounded by peach and apricot trees. What a pretty picture it all made.

"Let's have a little worship before heading on," Dad said. After reading a chapter from the book of Psalms, Dad prayed. "Dear Lord, thank you for your watch care through the night. Please be with us as we travel today. May we ever be faithful to you is my prayer, in Jesus' Name, Amen."

"Do you see a gentleman coming down the driveway?" Mom was asking. "He looks like he's coming to talk to us."

"Oh my. Is he going to scold us for sleeping on his property? I think I'll hide in the car." In a moment I was on the floor of the backseat of the car.

"Good morning, my friend. Did you have a good sleep?" I peeked out of the window of the car. Could this be the farmer who owns the pigs and fruit trees?

"We surely did, and we would like to thank you for providing the space." Dad was most gracious.

"I'm sorry that you didn't come up to the house. We would have given you a bedroom and comfortable beds." His eyes sparkled. "My wife sent me down here to tell you folks that breakfast will be served whenever you are ready."

"My goodness, you folks are so hospitable. We would love to join you."

Hurriedly we packed and were ready to be on our way. The farmer's wife was a sweet little lady, totally absorbed in making us comfortable.

I forget the menu of that special breakfast, but I shall forever remember the canned peaches from their orchard and the mouth melting biscuits that she served to us that day.

I don't believe that they had ever talked to anyone who had been so far away as India, and they were intrigued beyond belief by a firsthand account of our description of life in that far off land. Parting time came much too soon for both parties. In that short time these dear people had taken on the aura of "family" to us. And I am sure that they thought the same about us.

It was about six o'clock that evening. Dad was driving–Ted was sharing the front seat with him. Mom and I were enjoying the passing landscape from the backseat.

"Mom." Mom glanced over in my direction with an expectant look on her face.

"Yes, Honey. What can I do for you?" "Do you remember.....remember.....yeah, well .....do you remember once on the ship when I was missing India real much...... and....."

"And you were wondering if ever you would get to feel that way about America? Is that what you were wondering?"

"Yeah."

"How do you feel about it now?"

" Better. A lot better."

"Why is that?"

"'Cause.....well, you know how big white people have always scared me. And I was sure that I would always be afraid of them here. But if a lot of then turned out to be like the farmer and his wife then I'm O.K."

Mom scootched over to give me a big hug. We sat in silence for a few minutes.

"Is that all?" asked Mom, "so have you decided just what country is yours yet?"

"Yes. It'll always be India, but for a few years I'll just say that America is mine. And when I grow up and can do what I want to do, I'm going to go back to India and be a missionary."

AND I DID!!!!

Epilogue

God has always been the most important character in my life, and I wish to thank Him for the happy and fulfilling life that He has given to me.

No! It just can't be. It just can't. The years and years. Where have they gone? They have melded into memories-memories that I treasure so much today. In the preceding pages I have shared with you many of those thoughts from the long ago—like a story book half told. And now let me share with you the reality of today. The characters in this story...Where are they now? What did life face them with? Did they have families? Did they have careers? Now that you partially know them—I thought that some of the answers may be of interest to you.

Picking up the story from the night in Indiana, we made it to Walla Walla in record time. Following some initial contacts such as doctors—to check out my Mom—we were encouraged by their diagnosis. Following a few years of "build up," Mom could return to India and pick up where she had left off. How then do we spend the interval? It was decided that we would move to Loma Linda, California, and Dad would take the medical course at the Seventh-day Adventist Loma Linda University. Having seen the need for medical help in India, this solution greatly appealed to Dad.

One day in the process of growing up Ted was trying to get a reaction out of me - he decided to try by calling me a new name. How about Jerry Moon to rhyme with Mary June? That did it, and it's been Jerry ever since.

Again the years whizzed by, and Dad was asked by the Adventist church to return to India as a physician. There was one big problem...Ted and June! They were now adults working on their own careers—Ted in dental school and I in the nurse's course. Much as we hated to see our folks leave we knew that it was God's will for them to do so. Ted was now in the army—a soldier—and shortly he found a pretty little girl, Phyllis, also working on her career of nursing, and they were married. I too came across the love of my life, Stan, a soldier, and we were married.

Along about this time, word reached Mom and Dad that the Rajah of Teleprole had passed away. Their sorrow was etched with joy, however, when they heard that in his will he had left this short direction: *Do not bury me as a Hindu but rather as a Christian.*

My mother, the sweetest person on earth to me, came down with cancer. In four months she was gone! Gone! The sorrow was overwhelming.

In time Dad married again—her name was Vera. In a few years the General Conference asked Dad to be the director of its worldwide medical work of the church.

By now Stan was through with medical school (also at Loma Linda), and we elected to go as missionaries to Pakistan. The church had a new world-class hospital serving in the city of Karachi. It was there that we signed up for a full term of service which at that time was five years.

When we left the states we had three little ones: Rickey, Randy, and Ronnie. Later in Karachi three more came along: Rusty, Jim, and Jennie. (The last two were twins. Years before I had told my Mom that if ever I had a baby girl she would be named Jennie—after her). And what a joy she has been! Additionally, I have four delightful daughters-in-law — Susie, Janet, Cathy, and Lori Ann.

Those five years in Karachi were some of the happiest and fulfilling years of our lives. We would have returned in one year had it not been for our children's need of schooling. We settled in Yakima, Washington, where Stan built up a medical practice, and we built a home on a hill outside of town. There we planted a forty acre cherry orchard– that to keep the children busy. And there it is that we still call home.

In time, sixteen little grandchildren were added to our family: Rick's children - Shauna, Jenna and Trew; Randy's children - Shannon and Denver; Ron's children - Ryan, Eric and Amy; Russ's children - Riley, Landon, Sean and Anna; and Jim's children - Taylor, Savannah, Andrew and Parker.

My Dad passed away a number of years ago, and my Stan left us just two years past. We buried them both in Mt. Hope Cemetery, College Place, Washington. When I get too lonesome and sad I quickly remember God's promise that if faithful we will have the overwhelming joy of seeing them again.

Rick and Randy decided to follow in their Dad's footsteps by taking medicine. Ron, Rusty, and Jim decided on business. Jen took the nurse's course.

Ted–my brother –took dentistry and with that degree has gone to a number of countries carrying out not only dental care but also the story of Jesus. He is still in practice living in the town of Hermiston, Oregon, just one hundred miles away from where I live. He was happy to have three "little ones": Doug, Glenda and Dick. We are delighted that he is so close to us—making it often that we can get together.

Freddie went into farming in the state of Ohio. About ten years ago he became sick and passed away. He left two children to his heritage. Punkie passed away just four months ago. Her flock comprised one girl and three boys. She married a physician and spent the greater part of her life in the city of Corpus Christi, Texas.

God has always been the most important character in my life, and I wish to thank Him for the happy and fulfilling life that He has given to me. Thank you for reading my book. I do appreciate it.

Take care, and may God bless you.

Jerry

The Land My Childhood Knew

ISBN 978-1-935434-44-3

Mary June Flaiz Wilkinson

www.ingramcontent.com/pod-product-compliance
Lightning Source LLC
Chambersburg PA
CBHW030505100426
42813CB00002B/342

* 9 7 8 1 9 3 5 4 3 4 4 4 3 *